GOD SHED HIS GRACE ON ME

His Presence Is the Scarlet Thread
That Runs through the Pages of My Life
My Story

Linda Gundy George

ISBN 979-8-89428-646-4 (paperback)
ISBN 979-8-89428-647-1 (digital)

Christian Faith Publishing
832 Park Avenue
Meadville, PA 16335
www.christianfaithpublishing.com

Printed in the United States of America

Contents

Seasons of Life

There is a time for everything,
And a season for everything under heaven;
A time to be born and a time to die,
A time to plant and a time to uproot,
A time to kill and a time to heal,
A time to tear down and a time to build,
A time to weep and a time to laugh,
A time to mourn and a time to dance,
A time to scatter stones, and a time to gather them,
A time to embrace and a time to refrain,
A time to search and a time to give up,
A time to keep and a time to throw away,
A time to tear and a time to mend,
A time to be silent and a time to speak,
A time to love and a time to hate,
A time for war and a time for peace.

—Ecclesiastes 3:1–8

Preface

Life Has a Purpose

Your goodness and unfailing kindness shall
be with me all of my life, and afterwards I
will live with you forever in your home.
—Psalm 23:6 (TLB)

Life is a circle marked off in seasons. To every season, there is a purpose. And what that purpose is may take a lifetime to know or get right. This is my story, but in many ways, it may be a familiar theme that resonates with others whom God brought into this world for a reason. We are not an accident but uniquely made, with our own DNA to prove it.

I am writing this story because God asked me to do what He created me to do. He created me to glorify Him through the pages of this book. The trials and triumphant victories may resemble your personal experiences. Our life journeys have one thing in common: we're going somewhere, and how we go, forward or back, has a lot to do, as I've come to believe, with how well we listen to the voice of God. I didn't and paid the price, more than I was ever willing to pay. Negative consequences still raise their ugly regrets until my Savior reminds me of who I am and that He is working, regrets and all, into His perfect plan.

One thing I hope this story will do is show how much God loves us and that He is working all these ups and downs into something really good. Nothing is wasted. Yesterday, we faced the potholes and did the very thing we thought we would never do.

We are a work in progress. We are being made in His image. Now there's the rub. We don't look like what our Creator had in mind. At least, not yet. It's messy, but He knows the end from the beginning. He snips here and cuts there. Who can say, "What have You done?"

Some learn the lessons of life easier than others. Not me; I learn the hard way. I am the prodigal in Luke's story in chapter 15:11–32. Perhaps you learn that way too or are on the verge of taking off in that direction. If I could erase those years, I would. But I have learned from them. I have chosen to make the years ahead better because of them, not to waste life on things that don't matter, things that have no lasting value.

But my life story is His story because He is the Author of all the amazing things I have experienced. The ups are writing over the downs, and what He began in me is still being worked out according to His plan. His plan includes the time I was born, the people who were chosen to be my mom and dad, and the advantages and disadvantages that were woven into the storyline.

In hindsight, I would have changed things. I can't. But I can hope to show others how good God has always been to me. Through everything, He has been faithful. He knew me before I was even born and didn't pull the plug.

After this journey of life is through, I want to hear Him say to me, "Well done, my child, well done!"

Introduction

We will not hide them from their children
but tell to the coming generation the glorious
deeds of the LORD, and his might, and the
wonders that he has done. (Psalm 78:4)

I am writing this story for my children, my grandchildren, and my great-grandchildren. It is my prayer that they will be better moms and dads, better friends and neighbors, and better young people who will grow to become better old people. For they are leaving their own legacy for others to follow, and we all want to leave a good one.

For this is something I wish others had passed down to someone they may or may not have ever known. If I could pick up handwritten letters to me from my father, mother, grandparents, and even farther back, what a blessing that would be, one I would cherish forever, to hear in their own words the experiences that shaped their lives and what they learned from the good times and the difficult ones through their own eyes.

I would love to hear their personal stories—what they believed and not just what others said by painting them with the same broad brush. That is why I want to pass on my life in my own words.

For God shed His grace, and His blessings on me, and He wants me to bless my children and theirs for hopefully generations to come. What a joy it would be if something I said made a difference, and they passed it on.

I write for others who have known me, or maybe not. It would be an added blessing if you wrote your own story, as I have done from my heart. It is never too late to leave the legacy you want others to know, for nobody knows the real you but you—the you, you want others to know.

I also want those who follow me to know who I am and why I think as I do, what matters to me and why, and the lessons I've learned from Bible stories and how they apply to the lessons I have learned from my own experiences. I hope this will give you pause to think about how history does repeat itself. We can learn so much from the past of others. It is far easier to learn from others than to repeat some of the same dumb stuff.

I have tried to be accurate in how I remember people and events. I have tried to do my best to understand the feelings of others and how I portray them because their grace has covered me more than I care to admit.

God Shed His Grace on Me is also about making my Lord look good because He is!

And His presence is the Scarlet Thread that runs through the pages of my life.

Why Am I Here?

Why am I here? Does anyone know?
For a few short years, then it's time to go.
What is the point for me to be?
Is there a plan that's possible to see?
Am I one tiny strand in an overall plan,
Or a grain of sand in this vast land?

Who is this person I call me?
The reason I'm here, placed here in time.
The reason I breathe, think, love, and feel.
And when the allotted days of my life are no more,
And my worth on the earth has been given a score,
Will I win the approval of those whom I've loved?
Will I pass from this life with a yawn or applause?

But if the answer to this one single thread
Has a purpose beyond just the steps that I've tread,
A Designer who created each day for my good
And placed me exactly where He knew that I should.

The path that I journeyed, filled with so many mistakes,
I now see how everything I learned had a place,
And all an example of His mercy and grace.
To leave a legacy beyond these few short years
To those whom I have loved and hold so dear.

The Early Years

Planned in Advance

My frame was not hidden from you
when I was made in the secret place.
When I was woven together in the depths of
the earth, your eyes saw my unformed body.
All the days ordained for me were written in
your book before one of them came to be.
(Psalm 139:15–16 NIV)

I am not an accident, and neither are you. Each of us has a purpose and a place in this world. We were planned and wanted, and no two of us are the same. God knows the length of our lives, and nothing we do or fail to do is a surprise.

As a child, the first thing we learn is to trust. Our environment is safe and warm until a power surge happens when we have outgrown our allotted space in the womb. We have been pushing against this wall and then the other, but there is no room to get comfortable, and it's time to move out and move on, whether we are even aware of what is going on.

Our lives seem to be under the control of an eternal clock that says it's time or time's up. We don't control the button; in fact, we don't even know where it is. Perhaps if we knew what pressing it would cause, the pain that our next push would deliver, the mistakes and the consequences they would cause, we might say, "Hell no! We won't go!"

Just give us the battle plan so we can avoid the things we don't like and move on to our heavenly reward. But alas, we enter this world with blazing lights and noise. There are new sounds of yelling: "Do this. Do that!" Strange beings are waving, smiling, crying, and jumping up and down. This is our first day.

3

My purpose on my first day is to do good for the few short years that I am here. For God planned my life in advance, before I took my first breath. My life, from beginning to end, is all about trusting in Him to do His good will. That is also His purpose for you.

As I look over my life, I am able to see God's divine intervention. His presence is the Scarlet Thread that runs through the years. The parents He placed me with, the generation I grew up in, and the life experiences that affected who I am and what I believe today. This is my story; this is how God shed His grace on me.

I came into this world on the thirteenth of January. It was a Friday. I didn't wait for a day with fewer negative attachments. I had a future before me, and it was time to get going. I don't know if I was planned by Walter, my dad, and Lorine, my mother, but God knew just the right combination for a little girl like me. I was loved, nurtured, and accepted unconditionally—the perfect environment that every child needs.

The people who provided my happy home never had to learn to be content; they just were. The Depression was over, and it was a new day. Everything they needed, God had provided: the basics, food, water, and shelter, and everything else was cream on top of the milk—real blessings.

Looking back, I think we were poor, but we were just like our neighbors, so we never knew. Dad supplied our needs and occasional wants, and Mom stayed home because that's what moms did in the 1950s. She was content to do "mom" things, and Dad was the breadwinner.

In the fifties, milk and bread were delivered to our door, as well as handwritten letters. When I was sick, the doctor came to the house, and so did the neighbors. I lived on a Mr. Rogers neighborhood-looking street with a real sense of community. Everyone knew your name.

I attended Mark Twain Elementary School. It was typical to walk the twelve blocks of the familiar path with the kids in the neighborhood. Parents thought we needed exercise and opted out of bus service. We liked the sloppy joes and spaghetti red in the cafeteria, but most of the time, we took our paper sack lunches and carried two cents for milk money.

The policeman, Mr. Arborgas, helped us safely across the street when the bell rang to signal the end of the day. Since we lived about a mile away, it took close to an hour to get home. We frequently stopped along the way to buy a Cherry Coke or a sack of penny candy from the local "mom and pop" store. Once we finally arrived, we ran from backyard to backyard playing ball and hide and seek. There was plenty of good, clean fun for all to enjoy.

Summers in Kansas City, Missouri, were hot and humid. Kids didn't notice; that's the way it was in the Midwest in 1955. It would be years before air conditioning was considered a basic necessity and added to food, water, and shelter.

In those days, we were always on a bike or playing ball—rain or shine. I don't remember many times when we needed to wear shoes unless we were on our way to school or church. In fact, we were always outside unless our moms called us in for supper or we were sick. No one would be in front of a TV or video games. Transistor radios were a hot new item at the time. Roosevelt made radio popular before TV. Now Eisenhower was the voice of America.

Most parenting lectures were pretty much the same. Children were told about the dangers of strangers. We had to be home before dark and close enough to hear our mothers calling. Our moms and dads knew our friends' moms and dads. If we did anything wrong, they would tell our moms and dads. Yes, we all had *narrow-minded* parents who believed in right and wrong. And believe me, they knew it when they saw it. It was common knowledge in those days.

Mrs. Perry, my teacher in the second grade, began the day with the Pledge of Allegiance. We were "one nation under God." She would pray with us for our nation and would ask God to bless us and help us to become the people He created us to be. She was thankful for each one of us, and we loved and respected Mrs. Perry.

This was life as we commonly knew it. Parents lived at the same address with few exceptions. We attended church as a family and prayed before we ate, being thankful for all our many blessings. We waved flags and were proud of our country. This was who we were, and no one felt that there was anything wrong with this picture.

Memories of Mom and Dad

Children, obey your parents in the Lord, for this is right. "Honor your father and mother"—which is the first commandment with a promise—"that it may go well with you and that you may enjoy long life on the earth." (Ephesians 1:1–3)

The early years of my life are filled with wonderful memories of my parents, who loved each other and loved their children.

My mother was my first teacher. She didn't have a lot of formal education. The war was a real hardship for her family, and for one reason or another, she left school after the sixth grade. That was common in those days. But that only made her prouder of her three children. I knew that for me to be able to accomplish what she did not was enough. I suppose the bar of great accomplishments was set very low. I was never told, "You can do better," and in fact, when my grade card in elementary school said satisfactory, and I passed, that was great news.

Mom enjoyed her hobbies, like making quilts and embroidering. She even had time to make my clothes by hand. I never thought she did this to save money. She just had a real talent for making the tiniest stitches, and everything was beautiful and better made than the mail-order catalog clothes that came from Montgomery Ward.

She loved flowers and her flower gardens. When I came home from school, I could usually find her working on her flowers, gathering her own seed, and starting new plants. Many of the plants in her yard came from the local park. Every fall, they gave the plants and bulbs away to anyone who wanted to dig them up, so this became an annual event.

Every holiday seemed special because she made them special. In addition to major holidays, we celebrated the first day of May, appropriately called May Day. We gathered flowers from her gardens to put into handmade baskets to hang on our neighbors' doors.

When the Christmas season arrived, she loved decorating with all the holiday trimmings. Big red bells were strung from all four corners of the living room and tied in the middle by the biggest one of all.

Along with gardening, landscaping, decorating, and sewing, my mom was a good cook. Nothing fancy, but good home cooking. Pot roast on Sundays and the rest of the week always included meatloaf, pork chops, and even fried chicken, mashed potatoes, and real gravy. Fried was a staple. Those were the days!

Mom was a stay-at-home mom. Taking care of our family was her full-time job. But she earned extra money by taking in ironing on the days when things needed ironing. She also watched children whose mothers worked. They were the exception, not the rule.

There were always kids to play with around our house, and our home became like a second home to some who didn't want to leave at the end of the day. They loved my mom because she loved them. And she had time for them, just like my teacher, Mrs. Perry.

Things were changing in America. Where once we did without what we could not afford, we now joined the millions of Americans who owned a washing machine, television set, and a new car. The installment plan, in its beginning, seemed like a good plan, making the things we needed and wanted much easier to acquire. So like our neighbors, we were moving on up to the middle class.

But my dad never let debt get out of control. He weighed the cost of every decision, and if the purchase could wait, then it did. Delayed gratification was not taught as much as caught in those days.

Going through the hardships of the Depression taught men like my dad, and people in general, to use finances wisely and not throw stuff away. Being a strong believer in the *conservation movement* when it came to reusing, renewing, and recycling was a practice and not just a slogan. It was a good stewardship principle, and as simple as that.

Dad loved baseball. He loved the house he had designed and built himself for his family. He loved animals, gardens, fishing on the river, green fried tomatoes, and most of all, my mother. I don't think they ever argued, just like June and Ward Cleaver from the show *Leave It to Beaver*.

My dad was a quiet man. He taught me, without saying a word, about honesty, believing the best in others, and most of all, humility. He was loving, good-natured, and kind. He had a great sense of humor too.

I remember when the astronauts went to the moon, he made us moon rocks from some rocks he found in the backyard. We had our own moon rocks and our own pet rocks. We had a huge rope swing like Tarzan, and the neighborhood kids spent hours swinging back and forth through the trees.

My dad was the essence of God. He loved me and had time for me. He included me in the things he liked to do. He liked showing me off because he was proud to be my father. So the transition from making my daddy look good to making my God look good was part of God's future plans for me. I had a song to sing and a story to tell.

My Father's Example

Teach a child to choose the right path,
and when they are older they will remain
upon it. (Proverbs 22:6 TLB)

When I was a little girl, my daddy was the one who made the biggest impact on me. The little things that seemed so insignificant at the time shaped my character, who I would become, and most of all, my love and devotion to God.

Running to the end of the driveway, waiting anxiously for him to come down the road, was a four-o'clock ritual I did not want to miss. Same time every day, he would get out of the car carrying his lunch bucket after a hard day of work at an automobile plant assembly line.

I remember certain things like they happened only yesterday. I'm not seven anymore, but in my seventies. Strange thing about memories—big things may go right over a little girl's head, but a daddy's personal words of praise will be with her forever.

Another memory was a trip down a huge water slide into the deep waters below. Before we took the scary plunge into the dark abyss, Daddy's big, strong arms pushed me up high to keep my head from going under. Giggles removed fear, being safe in the arms of the one who loved me, the one I trusted.

The saying is true: we do not remember days; we remember moments. This moment of my childhood and others are engraved permanently on my heart, like Daddy, always playing the familiar fun game of who can get the lunch pail hidden behind his back. The game of dodge continued until he relinquished the treasure that often had a candy bar inside.

"Now how did that get in there?" he'd say. "Guess you'd better eat it, little girl, before it melts." And I pretended not to know who put it in there either.

My daddy was not much of a talker, but he didn't need to be. He showed love in everything he did. And everything he did made me feel loved. There was no doubt.

As a little girl, I always thought we were poor. And I guess if you judge those things according to what you have or have not, we were. But although we didn't get everything we wanted, we had everything we needed. I secretly wanted the latest toy like everyone else. Children didn't expect the hot item of the day, but Dad surprised me with a transistor radio that year that was new on the market. I couldn't believe we had that much money. But the message was greater than the gift wrapped in the box, expressing the love in his heart.

Remember this: it seems like today there is so much of everything that kids and adults have, but they hardly play with it before wanting the next latest new thing. The more we have, the more we want, addicted to having our stuff.

Now maybe these ramblings about my early years are not relevant to you, but if you're still with me, I do have a story to tell. If you're still reading along, I'll continue.

As I said at the beginning of this story, when I was a little girl, my daddy would be the one who made the biggest impact on my life. The unimportant things that seemed insignificant at the time shaped my character, shaped the person I would become, and most of all, shaped my love and devotion to God.

Every little girl needs to know her daddy loves her, and every little girl wants her daddy to be proud of her. My daddy was proud of me. He came from a family of nine brothers who were also raising their children, so everyone had a brood of kids to work on the farms.

In the fifties, times were different. A common saying in the day was children should be seen and not heard. But I guess to my daddy, that didn't apply. So whenever there would be any of those family members gathered around, he would pick me up and put me on a table to sing my heart out to Jesus. He would glow with pride over his cute little girl whom he loved.

The funny thing about memories are there are those that sticks out and those that we so easily forget. It doesn't have to cost a lot, and it doesn't have to mean a lot to anyone else, but little minds are recording volumes of information about their worth, like my daddy holding my hand, walking along the long, busy city sidewalk outside of the church where he faithfully served the God he loved. I was dressed in my pretty dress from the Montgomery Ward catalog and wearing new patent leather shoes.

He would pick me up and swing me over the puddles that I would, on an ordinary occasion, want to jump right in the middle of. But not on our special day. I needed to stay pretty because I knew my daddy was proud of me and liked to show and tell how much to anyone who happened to be around.

Whether he was taking me to the doctor to get shots when I had an infection that wouldn't go away, and there would be ice cream after the tears, or when I didn't want to eat certain vegetables and other yucky stuff, my daddy devised a plan of trickery to make it fun.

Daniel Boone was a TV show that was popular, and we watched it together and never missed an episode. Well, Daddy started the club, and to be in the Daniel Boone club, I ate carrots and green beans, and picked up toys and shoes.

I knew he loved me, and I knew he was proud of me. I knew I was so proud of him, and I looked up to him and loved him so much too.

Years later, that little church where my daddy served the God he loved told me how they would watch him slowly walk up that sidewalk. He slowly walked up that sidewalk carrying his Bible to teach a Sunday school class. He could not breathe well, and it was a struggle. But he would not have thought about not going. He loved them, and he loved teaching the Word of God.

He walked alone, no little girl beside him now, no one to pick up even if he'd had the strength to swing over the puddles or lift high out of the water to hear her giggles. Yes, the little girl who thought her daddy could walk on water—because he could. Life passes quickly. The moments we cherish are soon gone. The people we love are not with us forever. We grow up. We try to fix our own broken things, and walking around in Daddy's shoes gets harder and harder to do.

My father's life is woven into mine. It is a story that I want to leave to our family. This is a story perhaps much like your own, with exciting times and deeply regrettable ones too. My father was there for me through the years, the good ones, and the ones I wish I could erase.

The memories of my father will stay with me forever. He was perhaps the humblest of men. He liked being who he was and didn't need anything he didn't already have to be happy.

I remember the time when I was at the lowest point in my life; my mother and father came to the place where I worked to take me out to lunch. I could see my dad crossing the busy street wearing the hat I had given him for Christmas and the suit jacket of many colors I had made in high school home economics class. I watched him take my mother's arm and help her across the busy street, wearing the jacket that would stop the traffic.

I was so proud of my dad, who would rather wear something his daughter made for him, no matter how it looked or fit, than the best that money could buy. My dad was the image of God to me. I might forget the things he said, but I will never forget the image I have forever recorded in my mind.

The sweet, safe environment of my early years was beginning to change; styles and attitudes were progressing forward, and not in a good way. I was on my way home from school when I learned that someone had shot and killed our President, John Kennedy. The year was 1963. The pictures on the TV portrayed a different world than I had known.

The race riots in the late sixties were another example of the ugliness of human nature. Our neighborhood was mostly white until later when I went to high school. I never knew that white and black children were not supposed to go to school together, but I guess that was the attitude of many at the time.

I don't remember being around people who felt they were better than others, so if we were prejudiced, we couldn't see it. Besides, I knew God loved us all; we sang it on Sunday.

We were no longer content. Our nation was not united, and I am sure Mrs. Perry would agree that we had a lot to learn before we would be the people God created us to be.

School, Marriage, Work

My Changing World

But He knows the way I take; When He has tried me, I shall come forth as gold. (Job 23:10 NASB)

The year I graduated from high school brought even more change. But this time, the change was in me. I succeeded in overcoming my *satisfactory* report card label given to me in elementary school. Now I believed I could proceed into a destiny with amazing results.

Everything about life was fun, or I made it fun. I loved people, and everyone seemed to love me. I could talk my way out of troubles, or so I thought, and I had no time for gloom and doom. It was good to be alive and on my way to the future that Mrs. Perry had prepared us for.

Then I met someone who changed all that. He talked; I listened. He laughed at my naive thoughts and expected me to see life through his eyes, which I learned to do. He thought my friends were silly and immature, so he needed to exclude them from my life. We only did things he liked to do with the people he wanted in his life, which were not many. I had no friends of my own, and I had no life of my own.

I don't know why I gave him this control. It was a gradual change in our relationship, and fear of his sudden mood swings kept me from expressing how I felt. I made excuses for him. I wanted to believe that we could work our problems out. I protected him because I really thought, however naively, that I could change him.

But no one can change someone else. They must first take responsibility for their own actions and want help. Stop blaming other people for their unhappiness or playing the familiar game of "if only." We know it well. If only I had more money, better parents, the job they gave to someone else—just fill in the blank. The comparison trap is never satisfied. And another ugly truth is that it is hungry and grows. A word becomes an offense, and an offense becomes anger, and the anger becomes bitterness, and the bitterness erupts into rage at some point, and we were going in that direction.

I have always tried to look for the best in others, being part of their team and encouraging them to be all they could be. But instead of my unconditional love helping, I became part of the problem. I now know that God was warning me to get away from him, but my desire to make it work and my strong will to not give up made me stay. A nice sound to what really was only stubborn pride. I didn't want to admit to myself and to others that I made a mistake.

Soon after we were married, my life with this man was filled with terror that I had never known. There were many nights when he would pick me up from work with the obvious signs that he had been drinking, and far too much. The agony of knowing that we might be in a car wreck or, even worse, cause someone else to be injured or lose their life was unbearable. Of course, he would not listen to my anxious words and seemed to think scaring me was a fun game.

Trying to be quiet and not make things worse only made his immature and reckless behavior agitate him more. He was looking for an argument and someone to blame. His common complaint was that I thought I was better than him. I was once again being accused of looking for someone else. His jealousy was a constant turmoil for me.

I had done nothing to deserve his mental abuse. How could I defend myself from the unfair accusations? If I said the wrong thing, I was hit in the face by his uncontrolled rage. It took days for the black-and-blue marks to go away, and the emotional scars took years to heal.

There were times when the person I thought I knew could be fun to be with, and I would think that maybe we had turned the ugly corner. When he was working, we blended into my vision of a *normal* couple trying to live the American dream. But then, he would lose his job or quit, and this freedom always meant trouble.

One time, he took my paycheck and foolishly gambled it all away. Bills had to be paid. The character of my dad and the man I married could not have been more different. But I had to deal with what was before me now. Should I ask my father for money? What would I say? I never wanted my dad to know about the abuse or how irresponsible my decision to marry this man was. Now I know I was part of the problem. I was doing more than protecting him; I was enabling him to continue this degrading lifestyle. And, also, my pride kept me there.

We lived in the inner city. During the day, the surroundings were familiar, and dangers were minimal. But after dark, the neighborhood became a place of lurking dangers, some imagined, but many real. Feeling desperate, I ran from the house sometime between two and three in the morning, with only one thought: to get away.

I had no place to go and soon realized I had traded one dangerous situation for another. I started to panic. I had no money with me and, thinking back, probably not even my shoes. Fight or flight, and I chose to run.

I soon realized how foolish this night flight had become. I ran back to the house but with a determined spirit to do whatever I needed to do to escape the nightmare I was living. One night, I slept with a knife under my pillow. "No way he was going to hurt me again" sounded good, but I knew that the courage prop was not a deterrent in any way.

I remembered my mother saying a familiar saying of the day. I laughed at the thought that made no sense at the time, but now it did: "If you make your bed, you will have to lie in it." So here was the bed I made, and I was lying on it with a knife under my pillow. Not funny anymore. I was terrified of this person whom I had never really known.

I was not equipped to handle this. I was never meant to fix a broken world—not his, and not my own. I realized how far I had wandered away from the God I knew and loved. The things I had been taught by people who loved me filled me once again with the words of Jesus: "I will never leave you or forsake you. Cast your cares

17

on Me; Do not be anxious and afraid." Bible verses I learned as a child reassured me and gave my life value again. I felt the overwhelming power of His love.

I humbly turned to Him in a prayer, asking Him to help me. But even if the consequences of rebellion remained, I would not be alone. The promise I made was not dependent on anything other than the desire to live my life for Him. I needed Him; I wanted Him. I was truly the prodigal coming home.

From the depths of despair, O Lord, I call
for your help. Hear my cry, O Lord. Pay
attention to my prayer. (Psalm 130:1–2)

God moves in mysterious ways, but maybe not a mystery at all. The breakthrough, or turnaround, in my situation, came a few days later when he was put in jail for driving under the influence of alcohol charge. It was only a matter of time. It was also a good thing that there was nothing I could do to get him out of jail. For that, I was spared.

It was then that I learned about his girlfriend, or at least one of them. The current one called to inform me of the news, which I guess was intended to inflict more mental abuse. I only thought that if he had her, maybe he would leave me alone.

The power to control me with words or actions did not exist. And now, as I listened to the girlfriend on the phone, my emotions were numb. There was no love, and there was no hate. I didn't feel anything, and I wasn't sure if that was a good place to be.

It was hard for him to allow me to walk out of his life. He threatened me, again. He pleaded that he would change, again. He said that he was sorry and that he loved me, again. But I knew it was all meaningless words, again.

Jail would provide temporary safety and time to legally escape from this marriage. The first thing was to accept help from my dad and move back (rent-free) into the house and neighborhood where I grew up. Having a couple of my night shift coworkers live with me created the illusion of security. But even the restraining order that the attorney put on him to keep him away from me, I knew would not stop him. In my mind, I felt him waiting for me behind every bush and shadow, choosing the time when I would be the most vulnerable.

One night, after a fun evening with a group of friends, one new friend—a marine—and his comrade in the rice paddy battlefields of Vietnam made it their mission to scope out the territory known as my backyard. This maneuver to surprise a disgruntled, soon-to-be ex-husband was humorous. Funny because the only way the marine passed his physical to get into the military was by pressing buttons on his hearing test that he could not hear; his comrade was blind except for very thick glasses. Together, they searched the *jungles* around my house. Combat duty kicked into action, and these two, these proud few, were getting me through another day of enemy attack.

But the day I was most vulnerable did arrive. I was home alone that night. The mental abuse started all over again. He said he would change if I came back. He would kill himself if I didn't. Maybe hitting me repeatedly made him feel better about my wanting to leave, but it did nothing to make me want to return to the cycle of abuse.

"Killing himself would have been a good idea," the police officer said. My abuser had taken off as soon as my roommates came in and called them for help. A warrant was put out for his arrest. But after that night, he was gone from my life forever.

Because his life had no stability in it, it was impossible to know where he lived to serve him with the legal papers that would end the marriage. It took a long time, but eventually, he was notified in the newspaper of our divorce date. (He thought that my not being able to serve him with these papers would be one more act of power over me.) But he was wrong, and our divorce took place without him.

I have long ago forgiven him. He had so much to deal with that I hope he found peace in his own personal hell. He was abandoned by his mother, spent years in foster care, and was kicked out of the Navy. I believe he never knew how to love anyone, even himself. I would like to think he met that one person who could help him find the answer to his problems and help him find the plan God created for his life—to give him hope and a future. Maybe things could have been different if there had been a Mrs. Perry in his life or at the very least a mother.

Love is not control. It will not make someone feel scared or inferior. It will honor them, respect them, and encourage them to be the best they can be. It is not thinking about what they can get from someone, but what they can give. It is not selfish but would be willing to sacrifice their own wants for another. In fact, it would seem like no sacrifice at all but a gift.

Even when divorce is the only answer, the feeling of failure is like a sign that hangs around your neck. It takes time to heal the hurt and time to forgive—the other person and especially yourself. If this does not occur, the scars will never heal properly and will only affect other relationships, keeping the person in the bondage that was thought to be in their past.

We can't blame everything on someone else either. That's not productive. After all, we made the decision and perhaps ignored good advice or an inner voice of warning. We are responsible for our own actions, and we come into the relationship with our own set of faults. We learn, we grow, and then it's time to press on. It's not easy; change never is.

It seems to be inevitable, though, that we face the same stages as the one who goes through a death. We may blame ourselves, and go through a time of denial, hurt, anger, depression, and perhaps despair. But unlike the death of a loved one, there are few good memories. We may wonder if we could ever trust our feelings again or believe that someone who says they love us really loves us—ever again?

Starting Over

For I know the plans I have for you, plans
to prosper you, plans to prosper you and
not to hard you, plans to give you a hope
and a future. (Jeremiah 29:11)

My new friend, the marine, wanted me to call him when the divorce finally went through. I didn't know if I would ever see him again. Looking back to the day we first met, he had just arrived in town after leaving a war zone in Southeast Asia; right away, we had a lot in common. But the day I was finally free, he was there…waiting for me.

It was the beginning of a storybook romance. My handsome prince, wearing his dress blues, escorted me to that year's annual Marine Corps Ball. I wore a beautiful gown with slippers dyed to match. My hair was piled high in cascading curls, which gave the appearance of loveliness and grace. The evening felt as if it were magic. The night's enchantment lasted long after midnight as we laughed, danced, and fell in love.

Could my happiness be real or only a silly childhood dream? He said all the *right* words, his thoughtfulness was so appealing, and he made me feel safe. Yet I was determined not to make the same mistake—and that would take time, a lot of time. I knew what to look for; I was no longer naive and would not be deceived into believing something that probably wasn't true.

I tested him, tried to provoke him, and tried to bring out his worst side. But he took every challenge with patience and grace. I noticed qualities in him that resembled my dad, probably why they enjoyed being together and sharing their common interest in baseball. Soon my dad caught on to the love of football because of my marine. Parents are usually better at seeing things in the character of the one their children are dating. At least, it was for me.

My entire life lay before me. This time, God was leading, and I was following the way I should go. I had made the decision not to paint everyone with the same broad brush. This proved me right. I had given my handsome prince plenty of chances to turn this dream into what I prayed it would never be. He passed with flying colors, and we were married on June 26, 1971.

So with a kiss of luck, we were on our way. We took off for a honeymoon in the Colorado Rocky Mountains. I had been well-trained in my upbringing to live on a shoelace, and although I think we were poor, we never knew. We were content with the basics, and everything else was an added blessing.

That night was over fifty years ago; every day in some way, he demonstrates that dreams do come true. After all, only love would make someone who hates to cook move the TV station off ESPN to the Food Network station and spend all day preparing a special five-course Valentine's meal, including shopping, chopping, elegantly serving, and tirelessly cleaning everything up. But it is also bringing me a hot cup of coffee, knowing the one I have is not hot enough for me, or sitting in front of a fire with a glass of fine wine—listening, really listening to me.

But happily ever after, now that might be a stretch. After all, we are imperfect people living in an imperfect world. Falling in love is easy, but staying in love is a choice. And that kind of love is not a childhood dream, but a love that will last a lifetime, not a sacrifice at all, but a gift coming down from above. We learn to be thoughtful, we learn to be forgiving, and we learn to really love over time.

Love is patient, love is kind. It does not envy,
it does not boast, it is not proud. It is not rude,
it is not self-seeking, it is not easily angered,
it keeps no record of wrongs. Love does not
delight in evil but rejoices with the truth. It

always protects, always trusts, always hopes,
always perseveres. (1 Corinthians 13:4–7)

This is the Bible's definition of love, and who can say it any better than that?

New Life

God made my life complete when I placed all the pieces before Him.

*When I got my act together, he gave me
a fresh start. God rewrote the text of my
life when I opened the book of my heart
to his eyes. (Psalm 18:20–24 MSG)*

Growing up in a loving Christian home gave me an early opportunity to witness God's love for me. Although I never doubted the reality of Jesus Christ, the Son of God, He became more my parents' God than my own. I had asked Him to be my Savior, but now I needed to follow Him and make Him my Lord.

My husband, Don, believed in God and was eager to accept Him as his Lord and personal Savior. This was something very precious we had in common. Now God would lead us into the future that we would share. God had a plan for our lives, and we wanted to cooperate.

That future began with finding a church where we would be more intellectually and spiritually challenged. We were growing in our faith and in our awareness of Him in new and exciting ways. We taught Sunday school and youth groups. We thoroughly enjoyed being with children of all ages and being part of their fun.

My reason for wanting to be involved in the lives of these young people felt very personal. Maybe I could help someone not make the same mistakes that I had made, hopefully giving them the knowledge of Jesus that would keep them from wandering away from Him.

We had goals and plans. We wanted to heal the sick and raise the spiritually dead. We were hungry and thirsty for all that God wanted us to know about Him. Bible studies helped us grow in our faith and our awareness of His personal involvement in our lives. The opportunities for service through our church ministries were fun times and established lifetime friendships.

Our church family has always been important to us. By being with other Christians, we stayed focused on the things that mattered to us—things that are eternal—and were not distracted by the fruitless, temporal things of the world. We enjoyed being with others who shared our faith and loved the One we loved. Because of our relationship with Jesus Christ, we wanted to know Him more and experience the joy of His presence. Being with other Christians helped us stay focused on the things that mattered to us, things that are eternal, and not be distracted by the things of the world.

We also had full-time jobs. I worked for a mutual funds company in Kansas City. Don worked for the government, but this time as a civilian. He studied nights to earn a degree in computer science, which took ten years to complete. Thinking he might be a permanent part-time student, he received a job offer from an insurance company in the field he was studying.

This blessing helped us move into the middle class. We bought on the installment plan. We bought a house. We bought furniture. We bought a washing machine, a dryer, and a car. We worked hard to fulfill the American dream.

Another blessing for me was meeting my new six-year-old stepson. Although Gordon had a mother he loved very much, he made room for me too. I always wanted to be a mom, and for a few weeks in the summer, that's what I got to be. God truly had a plan for my life, and His plan included this little boy who called me Mom.

We didn't see him as often as we would have liked because he lived sixteen hundred miles away in Idaho. We always enjoyed those few weeks he spent with us. And for him, it was summer camp. But soon we would put him on the plane and send him back home. That looming thought was confirmed when one day he said to me, "But my mother misses me too." I knew he loved us, but he needed to go. In fact, no one understood that more. Every child needs a mother who they know needs them in their life. I really understood. But at the same time, I had to face the fact that being a mother did not look like part of God's plan.

But I could not willingly give up on that dream for my life. I was not a quitter. God said that He had a future for me. He had a future with hope. It was time to stand up to this new challenge that I faced. God had given me the courage to face the obstacles to my happiness before. I believed that once again, I would find His strength to face whatever was ahead.

My faith, which I learned as a child, was being challenged to go to a deeper level. And with that deeper commitment, I would be faced with some of my hardest disappointments. It was time to begin a new phase of my life, where I would be spiritually challenged.

Having Gordon in my life was a blessing that only God would know how much I needed. He filled a void, a dream I'd put on hold. God was in control, and I was discovering just how wonderful and frustrating that new life was about to become.

Making the Grade

I regretted passing up college after high school, so I decided to give it a try. I felt it was time to enroll in higher learning. Once again, I would be intellectually and spiritually challenged. The liberal arts degree, I was told, would make me *well-rounded*; instead, I thought to myself, destined to turn me into a *liberal*.

I enjoyed my classes, which I combined with my full-time job. I studied hard and found thinking fun. I got excellent grades; therefore, I was asked to join a sorority for the students who studied hard and got excellent grades.

I learned how different people think and had a few opinions of my own. Most of the content was social engineering babble, but I was not so impressionable now. I had learned to think on my own. The mental torture from my first marriage would not allow me to let someone else do all the talking and thinking for me. By this time, I developed my own views and found an endless opportunity to articulate the fine art of dissent.

I didn't need to be told about good stewardship of Mother Nature or that some people don't like Black people. I heard at college that God had died in the '60s and that intelligent people without God could solve the problems of the world. It was basically "just be nice." I thought God had said that first when He said to love one another. And when we love one another, we naturally must be nice to one another. Anyway, I was fascinated with everything that contradicted my views. It made me think and equipped me to defend my beliefs.

Most of the time, the teachers respected the students who had different opinions and could articulate them. One time, I took the opportunity to stand up for the unborn. I volunteered to read my arguments on overpopulation and abortion *rights* to the class. I concluded my opinion by using the teacher's argument against him. I said that I thought we were a selfish population to put our own ambitions ahead of the next generation. He asked me what I thought my grade should be. I was smart enough to say an "A." That is what he gave me.

I graduated with flying colors and moved on to a four-year university. This new environment would not easily accept me. I was no longer an adult attending school at night with other adults. I was a nontraditional student sitting with the young, the impressionable, and the naive.

From the first day, I wondered if these people had been stuck in the '60s. The professors were still fighting the Vietnam War from the safety of the classroom; all they lacked were their protest signs, and their lives would have a purpose. I thought they should move on.

I learned a lot about people, though. After working for what seemed like forever on a paper, trying to make it perfect, I lost two grade points because it was four words too many. I know rules are rules, but I missed their point. I felt like starting a war but decided to listen to my own advice and move on.

I soon learned how to get with their program. I knew how to answer the questions according to their "truth" and tell them what they wanted to hear. But when God was being blamed for things He didn't do, I felt someone should say something, and that was usually me. It never made sense to me for people to say that God does not exist, and then blame Him for everything that's wrong in the world.

In fact, people seem to fight their biggest battle over things they say they don't believe. If God does not exist as they claim, why even bring Him up at all? I think it is because they can't explain the reason they exist without believing in God. But that is their battle, not mine.

Working a full-time job and taking classes temporarily distracted my mind from thinking about what I wanted most: being a mom. It was becoming evident that this was the hardest test that I would ever have to pass. I was about to face years of infertility. Years of struggling with a life of contentment being waged on the battlefield of my mind. Years of praying for the answer that never came and not knowing why.

Heartache

He heals the heartbroken and bandages their
wounds. He counts the stars and assigns each
a name. Our Lord is great, with limitless
strength; we'll never comprehend what he
knows and does. (Psalm 147:3–5 MSG)

The heartache of wanting to have a baby left me constantly disappointed. I attended the baby showers of others and did my best to be part of the team that planned and produced the beautiful, happy celebrations for so many others. Mother's Day was becoming something I would dread.

Medical science has been able to help many with infertility problems, but in the 1970s, that was not the case. I was before *test-tube* babies, and my options were limited, even though my doctor was considered one of the best in his field at one of the best teaching hospitals in the country.

I was determined to try any test and endless procedure—but to no avail. I waited hours in doctors' offices with all the very pregnant mothers-to-be. The fight to overcome and the financial expense never brought my dream any closer. Was it time for me to put that dream aside? Never!

I picked up the magazine on potty training and waited my turn to see the doctor. The time passed slowly, and my thoughts were speeding up. I grew more anxious the longer it took.

The test results were not good. I was told that my fallopian tubes were blocked. The cause he did not know. He explained a new experimental procedure that offered the hope that I so desperately wanted. There was only a 10 percent chance of this being successful, but all I wanted to hear was that there was a chance. I knew this was my one and only remote possibility of ever being able to conceive.

For six weeks I wore artificial tubes inside my damaged ones to prop them open. I changed the messy bandages daily and saw it as a necessary inconvenience. My marine had slept on the hard floor by the side of the bed when I came home from the hospital. He thought I might need him. He didn't want to accidentally cause any damage to the tubes that were surgically implanted.

The day Dr. Cameron told me I was pregnant, I was ecstatic! I thought of nothing else. I daydreamed about the future and found it difficult to concentrate on anything else. But in a few weeks, something went wrong; I would double over in pain. The physical pain was nothing compared to the battle going on in my heart. I didn't want to go to the hospital; they might have told me what I didn't want to hear. Only God could stop the fear that controlled me, and I felt so alone.

My faith was being tested. I was being challenged to believe that God loved me despite taking away what I wanted most. If He were personally involved in my life, why wouldn't He make this nightmare go away?

"Although you are pregnant," the night shift doctors said, "the pregnancy is developing in the better tube." Of course, they would repair the damage to the remaining tube if they could, but they were not optimistic. No was not an option for me. I was numb. I didn't want to believe that what they were saying was true.

I signed the necessary paperwork to eliminate any legal messes that could arise, and immediately they ordered the surgery to fix my *problem*. The baby I carried would never be part of our lives, and the dream of holding this little one that I named Hannah Grace would forever be in my heart.

The next day, I learned that there was no way to save my fallopian tubes. The doctors had to remove both of them. They explained that if they had left even the better tube in, the risk of having this happen again was certain. So I was now faced with what was written in my medical file: pregnancy impossible.

God says a lot in a moment, like a wrinkle in time when a whole life is flashed before me. All the negative messages that God doesn't care, that He cannot be trusted with our dreams. These thoughts played over and over as I tried to make sense of what had happened. Surely His promises are meant for others; you are not special, you came into this world satisfactorily, and you have lived up to your calling.

The overwhelming feeling of being the one who sits outside the door, listening to the party, listening to the happiness of others but never meant to enter in. Voted less likely to succeed at anything that could be useful or fruitful for God to bless. The not-for-me messages pounding in my head.

Well, I could believe that about me, I could believe that about God, or I could choose to trust Him. Somehow I would not let this devastating news keep me from believing that there must be more.

Getting On with Life

The Lord is close to the brokenhearted and saves
those who are crushed in spirit. (Psalm 34:17)

We had hoped and prayed that the operation would be successful and give us the baby we longed for. That did not happen. But I had the love and support of Don, who helped me through the next day and the one after that. He was my husband and my friend. I needed him. He was my comfort through another disappointment; he listened when I needed to talk, and when I didn't feel I could, he answered the phone and relayed the prayers and concerns of those who loved me. He was my encouragement and my strength when I was weak. If I could feel, maybe I could live beyond this. I didn't know and didn't know if even time could answer that for me.

We had each other, and I needed to believe that was enough. I would learn to be content. I had the basics, and everything else was not part of God's plan. It had been my plan, my future, my hope—but not God's. He had another purpose for my life, and whatever that was, I reluctantly needed to find out.

After a time of mourning over what was not to be, I prayed myself out of the depression that consumed my life. I returned the many calls to family and friends, and with their help, rejoined the living. Some of my greatest experiences and friendships developed around this small community church where we belonged. We spent hours and many weekends together. Decades later, I remember those camping and canoeing trips down the *rapids* of the Missouri River. The point was not to tame the river but to eat a lot, laugh a lot, and enjoy life despite the rain.

One such adventure, we experienced was camping in a downpour and eating cold hotdogs and marshmallows. We were soaked to the bone, and so were the matches to light the fire. Another great time, that could only be fully appreciated after the danger had passed, was coming home from a ski trip in the worst snowstorm in history.

Crossing the open range of Kansas, we were one of many cars and vans that inched along ever so slowly when the highway department closed the road. "No way to get through," they said, and no motel with any vacancies we were finding out. But as God was with us, we found a motel with two rooms that had been closed or condemned, and we happily piled inside.

I do believe some of us slept a little, but it was hard to tell. We quieted down long enough to almost fall asleep. Then someone else would start to giggle, and it would spread around the room like a contagious disease. We remembered how Cramer was driving cautiously, wearing his ski goggles through the white and drifting snow, just to keep the van on what we thought was the road.

The whole room would roar when we replayed the trip up to the door of the last two remaining rooms in Kansas. It opened, and I let out a blood-curdling scream as I looked into the eyes of a wolflike man. My imagination was on steroids. I am sure he was more terrified of me as he bolted past me into the wilderness of snow.

Once we checked in, we soon discovered that one of our rooms was too hot, and the other was too cold. The radiator was noisy, and someone would need to get up every so often and bang on it to make it shut up. We were told not to open the refrigerator, which none of us wanted to do. We decided right then and there that the AAA rating on the sign-out front was terribly misleading.

Attitude of Expectancy

*Now faith is the assurance of things hoped for, the
conviction of things not seen. (Hebrews 11:1)*

We were halfway to Colorado before someone said, "Does anyone
know how to ski?"

Good question, I thought. Positive thinking took over, and we
were good to go. We had an attitude of expectancy that said if we
wanted something badly enough, it would happen.

The first thing on our agenda was to get our group organized
and enrolled in ski school. There would be plenty of time to conquer
the mountain, but first things first. So dressed in bargain basement
specials, we set out for snow bunny school. Some of us were quick to
learn; others were not, I being in the latter. We practiced stop and go,
walking up the mountain sideways, and snow plowing down. After
a good while of squatting on our skis, we slowly began to straighten
up. Then it was ski lift time; time to ski or cut rope.

Everyone fell down; there was no shame in that. Even when the
entire mountain shut down so I could get on the ski lift, it was still
okay. But once you boarded the chair and the iron bar trapped you
in, there was only one way to come down. It was common knowledge that coming down the mountain on the chair was the height of
humiliation. You had to come down the best way you could, be it on
skis or on your butt, which I was prepared to do.

We stayed on the bunny trails pretty much the whole day and
had a great time. We became skillful in the art of falling over and
popping up again. Most of the falls we took happened just by standing still and getting our ski tips tangled up with our own or someone
else's skis. But we were having a wonderful time out in God's country. We thought everything was hilarious, and everything was. We

35

noticed that other skiers were far above us, somewhere out there or up there, but we had no need to join them; we were content.

Nothing stays the same, though, and the very next day, the ski instructor advised me that I knew just enough to kill myself. Well, I was far more mad than afraid, so I would ski and prove him wrong.

The only one of us who had arrived in Colorado ski country and knew how to ski took me up with him to help me learn to conquer the snow. He pointed out the beautiful snow-covered trees as we rode up the side of the mountain, excited and united in one purpose: to have a good time. The sky was a brilliant blue, and we were almost rocked to sleep under its gorgeous canopy. Up and up we climbed. Looking out from the safety of the gondola, we could see the skiers right under our mode of transport, also enjoying their ride over the snow. Then it hit me: we were approaching the top of the world, and it was time to get off.

With ski tips up, we prepared to unload. I realized at that point there was no turning back. No guts, no glory.

Looking down at the mountain was enough to make you wish you were dead. *But just give it time*, I thought, and I would be. The curse of the bunny school instructor was about to come true. I was scared—no, I was terrified! The temptation to have a little fun soon disappeared as I faced the looming consequences: major breakage of body parts on the way down.

My friend, noticing the look of *green* on my face, advised me to ski over to him some distance away. *I could do that*, I thought, and besides, he was my lifeline to the bottom and would not get away, I assured myself.

"Don't look down," he said.

"Too late," I replied.

He said, "Just focus across the mountain over to the trees where we will be out of everyone else's way."

I could do that because I had done it before at the bottom of the mountain. Now he advised me to lean on my downhill ski. I began to turn ever so slowly and see what he directed me to—another safe forest of trees.

Off I went again in search of the "Holy Grail" or level ground, whichever. Before long, I would pick up speed and lean on my downhill ski to slow me down, but then move out to enjoy the sound of my skis flying across the snow.

The advice that I received that day was as if it came from God. I was told not to look down because it would be too frightening. I was advised to take one step or one small glide forward. I could rest when I got tired and always stay focused on the one up ahead who would be there to help me along.

My instructor, my guide, and my friend encouraged me to turn and look up. And what I could see was where I had been; I had unknowingly skied down the mountain. I had overcome the obstacles—the obstacle of fear, the obstacle of low expectations, and the fear of failure. I was a skier. I had earned my right to be on that mountain. I would never be the same, not only in this but also in all my challenges ahead.

Skiing became the one athletic thing that I could do, and I could do it well. I no longer skied on the bunny trails with the beginners but skied on advanced slopes, and a time or two, got myself off the black diamonds that accidentally crossed my path. These were great times for me, and I found myself waiting on others instead of others waiting on me.

This experience was a reminder that anything worth having or doing may not be so easy. I would listen to His voice, follow Him, and get out of everyone else's way. When I was exhausted, I had to rest and lean on His presence to give me the confidence to succeed. And if I fell or didn't get it exactly right, He would help me up. Falling is okay, but getting back up is my only option.

I would just keep working toward my dream, my dream of being a mother, no matter how impossible that would be. I would have an attitude of belief—a belief that by taking my life one day at a time, one step at a time, I would overcome with God as my instructor, the fear of never having that dream come true.

Skiing taught me many things about how to deal with the agony of defeat. I would pop back up ever so slowly and try again. I believe that it doesn't matter how many times we fall but that getting back up is our only option.

I have happy memories of those ski trips when we would pile into vans on a Friday night, drive across Missouri and Kansas to arrive at the peak of dawn, eat breakfast, and hit the ski slopes in Colorado without sleep. We would ski all day in groups or two by twos. Then we would have a quick dinner and hit the sack exhausted, only to do the same the next day, pile back into the caravan, and drive all night to return to work on Monday.

We considered any excuse to get together a high priority. Word of mouth was all that was required to fill our houses with friends, food, and laughter to boot.

Another great time for all of us was the annual prayer retreats at the lake. Women of all ages gathered together for a weekend of fun. It was a time of sharing our needs and concerns. The older women would nurture and help the younger women grow in their faith as we studied the Bible together.

We made a prayer list each year and crossed off the answers to those prayers the following year. What encouragement they were to me. And what hope they gave to me asking God to bless me with a child. There seemed to be no limit to their patience or what they felt God would do. Their love and support never wavered, and those times in my early years helped develop my growing faith in women who had faced the challenges of life and persevered.

And perseverance is learned from going through the test.

Although I had a great life that I enjoyed very much, the thought of not being able to have a child was forever there to remind me of what I had lost. For example, for some reason, everyone I worked with was in some stage of pregnancy. The subject of conversation was always about motherhood. No one could imagine the hurt that I felt they were causing me.

Gradually, I began to think about adoption. It probably started when a friend at work began the process but found that they too would be having a baby at the same time. This was too much. I began once again to chase the dream of being a mom, which I always wanted.

Anything worth having in life is worth whatever it takes, no matter how difficult or impossible that might be. That was my motto, and I was living it out.

At least, if the only thing I could control was my attitude, then I would have an attitude of expectancy. I would expect good things, and when hit with setbacks, go another way. I would not give up or give in. And for some reason, that I could not know then, God would not let me give up on my dream.

The steadfast love of the Lord never ceases,
his mercies never come to an end; they are
new every morning; great is your faithfulness.
(Lamentations 3:22–23 NRSV)

New Trail, New Trial

What a God! His road stretches straight and
smooth. Every God-direction is road-tested.
Everyone who runs toward him makes it. Is there
any god like God? (Psalm 18:30–31 MSG)

We met my stepson as he arrived on the plane for a ski trip in the Rockies. It didn't take him long to learn how to ski, and after a few hours, he joined us on the mountain. We got our trail maps out at lunch and planned our afternoon routes. Since we were meeting periodically to change partners so we could all ski together and learn from each other, it was important to know where to meet. There was always the risk that one of us would end up on "Oh no," and we might have to wait a while.

Once we were all accounted for, a self-appointed leader would usually emerge. Our destination flight plan was put into action with the shout to "follow the bumblebee," which was easy to spot on white snow. This bargain basement special ski coat was more than cheap; it was a beacon to point the way.

All vacations eventually come to an end, and then life goes back to normal. On Monday morning, my friend and coworker, the one who was pregnant and adopting a child, asked me if I had considered adoption. A social worker at her church found homes for babies of unwed mothers, and she might be able to help me. Of course, she didn't have any babies at the time, but she would pass our name on to her friend and let me know.

We had already started the long and tedious process of adoption a few years earlier and had found this too more difficult than we thought. We eagerly filled out all the applications placed before us. But we soon discovered that our name would be placed only on a waiting list and not the actual list. This, we were told, could take seven to ten additional years. Abortion was the reason given for why there were so few babies born and available to the thousands of couples who wanted them.

Then we found another obstacle. The agency had to be very selective in choosing prospective parents. We were not eligible if we had been previously married or if we already had a child; even a step-child would eliminate us. This proved devastating for me because we were guilty on both counts. It wasn't fair, I thought, but babies available for adoption were limited.

They thought they had a point, but I didn't. I only got to be a mother for a few weeks in the summer. Adopting a baby was once again proving impossible in this new day of *choice*.

Then the phone rang, and it was the social worker with good news. She was working with an unmarried couple who wanted to place their baby in a loving home. They requested that each of the five couples who wanted to be considered write a letter to them saying why they wanted to adopt their baby. My husband wrote his, and I wrote mine, and then we waited.

We were so happy when we learned that both the mother and the father had chosen us to be the ones who would best fulfill their desires. Since I had so much to look forward to, I panicked and went shopping! I needed everything—a nursery was about to be born. I floated from store to store for adorable baby clothes and the high-est-rated baby bed.

I would spend hours with bestselling children's books, enjoy-ing the world through the eyes of a child where animals talked and taught valuable lessons on being kind, sharing, and telling the truth. These lessons we all need to relearn from time to time.

I began the process of soaking up all I needed to know. It was becoming clear that being a great mom might be a little more com-plicated than I had first believed. Although the time went by so slowly, the day would soon arrive when we would pay the medical expenses and the attorney fee and then, we would have everything we ever wanted to be happy.

Our baby girl arrived early, weighing only four pounds. Since all the legal papers could not be signed due to the Thanksgiving holiday, we would have to wait. It would be a few days for this precious little girl to gain the extra weight she needed in order to leave the hospital. We were told that on Monday we would meet with the attorney and sign the documents.

The social worker and the hospital staff filled us in on her health and when we could expect her weight to be where she would be able to leave the hospital and come home. This happy event was another in their normal day, but for me, it was the beginning of the life I had always wanted.

But she never did come home to our home. By Monday morning, her birth mother found that she was unable to do what she had planned for months to do. It had nothing to do with how she felt about us; that had not changed, but she had changed.

How could I blame her? In fact, I may have been too good at explaining why I wanted to be a mother and why I wanted to have a baby to share my life. How could I not understand how she must have felt holding that precious little one's hand and looking with pride at the new little life she held? I understood, but it didn't make it easier. It was as if a part of me had died.

Would I be able to pick myself up after this fall? This obstacle was more than I was able to have a positive attitude about. I was crushed and heartbroken, and I was sure the future was as dark as I imagined.

A Time to Mourn, a Time to Dance

To everything there is a season and a time for every
purpose under heaven. (Ecclesiastes 3:1 NIV)

It's the first of March. All the trees looked dead, but that was only how they looked. God was actually preparing the world to reappear with all its colors and remove the bleak black and white. Soon, nature would be transformed, and all would be sunny and bright. But as for me, the future that stretched out before me remained dark.

I had been slow to put away the last of what was Christmas, and soon it would be Easter. I was reminded that everything has a season: a season of birth, a season of death, and then a season of rebirth. But in every season, there is a time out, a time of waiting for what we cannot see, a time to signal to all those around us that God takes care of His creation. New life was sprouting up through the snow from the bulbs I had planted in the fall, and the birds sang their songs as they built their nests. Life goes on.

I grieved over the death of my dream. It felt like the final blow to keep me down. The kick in the stomach was more than I could handle. Just moving from one chair to another took more energy than I seemed to have. I didn't see the point. If life had to go on, then it could go on without me. I was depressed, and staying there was okay with me.

I was moving into another stage of the grieving process: anger. How could God love me and let me hurt like this? Where was He, and did He care? But soon, I drew close to Him, seeking the comfort that I knew only He could give.

Recorded in my journal, I wrote:

"All the faith and optimism I had yesterday is gone. You said Your strength is made perfect in my weakness, and I have never felt so weak."

I was wrestling with what God wanted me to gain from all this hurt. My thoughts turned to the Scriptures. Bible verses that I had memorized over the years flooded my mind and began to help me accept and trust Him with all the things I could not understand. It was like a tape recorder playing words of encouragement to override the natural pessimistic way of looking at life's disappointments.

I had to ask myself why I followed Jesus. To be honest, was it for the things He did for me? A fair-weather Christian? *I will follow You, if and only* type of shallow belief. That was why many left Jesus in the final days of His ministry. His words were too hard and difficult to keep. They loved a prosperity gospel. They wanted power in the new kingdom, but not one of hardship, persecution, and pain. So they turned back.

> *Jesus asked his twelve followers, "You do not want to leave me too, do you?" Simon Peter answered him, "Lord, to whom shall we go? You have the words of eternal life. We believe and know that you are the Holy One of God." (John 6:66–68)*

This always tugged at my heart. Would I leave Him when life did not resemble what I had in mind? Would I leave Him when the answers to my prayers seemed to be no?

When John the Baptist was in prison and waiting to die, he questioned his commitment to Jesus. He wanted to know if Jesus was who He said He was, the one who came to set us free. Jesus answered and said for His disciples to tell John about all they heard and saw. The blind received sight, the lame walked, those who had leprosy were cured, the deaf heard, the dead were raised, and the good news was preached to the poor (Matthew 11:5).

Jesus did many miracles among the people to testify that He was the long-awaited Messiah, yet He did not deliver John from prison or death. Jesus answered his question and also mine. We will face hardships, and there are times we won't understand, but to the disciples and to you and me, He says,

Blessed is the one who does not fall away
on account of me. (Matthew 11:2–6)

And this was the kind of follower I knew I wanted to be.

God comforted me by providing the loving support of family and friends and a husband who waited on me literally hand and foot. The cards, letters, and phone calls encouraged me and meant so much. In this new season of my life, I recommitted my life to Him and to loving Him with all my heart.

In time, I came out of the depression, and life was given another chance. I would be content with today and leave my tomorrow in His hands. God was restoring my soul, renewing my mind, and pulling me up off the floor.

Forget Your Troubles, Choose Happy

*God gives gladness instead of sorrow and praise
instead of fainting. Weeping endures for a
night, but He gives the joy that comes in the
morning. He will comfort all who mourn and
provide for those who grieve, bestowing on them
a crown of beauty instead of ashes, gladness
instead of mourning, and a garment of praise
instead of despair. They will be called righteous,
and a planting of the Lord for the display of
His splendor (Psalm 30:5b, Isaiah 61:3b).*

*Above all else, guard your heart, for it is
the wellspring of life. (Proverbs 4:23)*

One of the gifts that God has given me to fight the enemy of my emotions is my sense of humor. I love to laugh. God would bring to my mind things out of the blue that would crack me up. Just out of the blue, someone would mention our first ski trip to Colorado when we stayed at the YMCA of the Rockies, which was very affordable for our budget. Immediately, we would go into the Village People's rendition of "Young Men…staying at the YMCA." It always made us roar with laughter.

My marine and I were enjoying the days and years ahead. When he asked me to marry him and live my life with him, we did not know what the future would be, but we had each other, and that was enough. I would be able to hope again because someone loved me and believed in me, and he made me laugh…the basics and everything else were real blessings.

This was a new day. I was determined to put yesterday behind me. I would keep my commitment to stay far away from situations that would destroy my positive outlook. I reminded myself that I didn't need anything I didn't already have to make me happy. But we did live in the real world, so maybe a bigger house was a good place to begin.

We found the perfect house to build, close to work and worship. We were busy with jobs, school, travel, and keeping up with the neighbors. It was the true American dream.

Then shortly after we moved into our beautiful new home in our lovely new neighborhood, I was pleasantly surprised on my return home to find a sign in my yard. I turned the corner to see a fairly good sketch resembling my house standing on the lawn. The invitation in bold letters invited me to a housewarming in my honor by the people who loved me. What a nice thing for my friends to do, right out of the blue.

They had planned everything. The food, the gifts, and the laughs were so welcomed. Good times. It was not a baby shower, but their expressions of love for us. We had wonderful friends, a lovely home, and a promising future.

But while driving the shoreline of Monterey, California, on my husband's business trip, that old familiar feeling of emptiness came over me again. For some reason, my mind was replaying the words in the doctor's office telling me that I would never be able to have a child. There was no emotion in his voice. It was his medical opinion; it was reality, and it hurt so much.

Driving along the beauty of the coastline that God had created made me ache once again for the baby I could not have. It was like time stood still, and pretending that I was accepting the news and getting on with life was not working. I could not snap out of this. I could not buy something to replace my dream, and no amount of positive pep talks would help me before the sadness took over once again.

Why would God not take the desire away? Must I live my life, always being reminded of what I have lost? I thought I had made peace with this, but here it was again. I needed what only God could give and completely find contentment in Him.

> *The Lord is my Shepherd. I have everything*
> *I need. He lets me rest in green meadows; he*
> *leads me beside peaceful streams. He renews my*
> *strength. He guides me along the right paths*
> *bringing honor to his name. (Psalm 23:1–3)*

I held on to this verse, determined to trust in His love for me. It was more than how I felt; it was a decision.

> *Now faith is being sure of what we hope for and*
> *certain of what we do not see. (Hebrews 11:4)*

Like the heroes of faith in the Bible, the ones that I wanted to pattern my life after when put to the test, were faithful. My future belonged to the unknown will of God. Where that would lead, I didn't have a clue.

Once again, I depended on the loving support God provided me through my family and friends. When I needed a hug or a laugh, someone was there.

The season was changing. The leaves were displaying their riot of colors for our enjoyment as we drove out to Karen's dad's farm. We climbed into the back of the wagon as he pulled our Sunday school young adult group around the back roads. The stars delighted us with their presence, and we showed our appreciation by singing, laughing, and praising God. We were kids again. We roasted hot dogs in the bonfire, huddling close to the burning embers to keep warm. There were stories to tell and memories to be made. Then it was time to get the kids back in the cars at the end of a fun Saturday.

I loved our day trips too. Karen, Suzanne, Pat, Sharon, and I would meet in the morning to shop, eat lunch, and catch up on the latest happenings. We took weekend trips together, enjoying Swedish culture, quaint little towns, and Amish communities. We talked nonstop, and whenever there was a gap in the conversation, someone would quickly fill it in. We drank tea and ate pastries, shopped for the latest *must-have* things, and returned home with our treasures and memories that one day someone like me would be writing about.

I was living a wonderful life. I chose to be happy; I chose to be grateful. I chose not to listen to the garbage of unbelief that might be dumped into my ears. I would recognize complaining and doubt as poison and not participate. I would see everything as an opportunity for God to perform a miracle, starting with me.

And then it was putting that good pep talk into the rest of the hours of the day.

A Whole New Life

Teaching from Experience

Those who plant in tears will harvest with
shouts of joy. (Psalm 126:5 NIV)

I thought everything in life was going pretty well. I had a devoted husband and a stepson who loved me and included me in his life. I had a good job and tons of friends. I enjoyed numerous hobbies and sought out new interests, determined not to be bored. When that happened, shopping filled the gap. We were at a place in our lives where we could afford our needs and wants, or at least in the near future. So what was the problem?

I couldn't put my finger on it. The desire to have a child would not go away. I could cover it up. I could distract myself with other things. I could stay busy and try to ignore the life that could have been. I pleaded with God to remove the desire to have a child. Surely, this made sense. After all, I needed to get on with the life I was meant to live. If there is life after death, then there must be life after the death of a dream.

Following the steps of my dad, I taught the Word of God in a weekly Sunday school class at the church we attended. I wanted these young girls to know the God I knew, the one I believed in, and the one who could do what He said He could do. They listened intently as I told them that God loves them and has a wonderful plan for their lives. I encouraged them to commit their lives to Him. He would guide them to make wise decisions and direct their paths. Studying the lives of Bible characters encourages us when we face life's challenges and hopefully helps us avoid repeating the costly mistakes made by others. I also used my own personal stories to illustrate the lesson for the day.

God had a purpose in the trials of those we read about. What we learn from them will help us become victorious in our life experiences too. Most of these girls came from Christian homes and regularly attended church. They attended all the programs offered by our church, like vacation Bible school, youth camps, and retreats. Their parents lived these principles and set a good example for them to follow. So what I was saying was not new—a kind of groupthink that had not personally been challenged or put to the test by a different worldview. They fit in and were comfortable in their environment, in a safe zone where they didn't know others who would lead them off God's path.

They were me at that age. Oh, how life has a way of making us prove what we say we believe. It is the story that goes back to the beginning, the beginning of time. I used Adam and Eve to make the point that their disobedience is repeated throughout history.

In the garden that God created, everything was perfect, all needs were met, and whatever we wanted was within our reach. We were content, we were comfortable, we didn't even know that there was something more. Because there wasn't; we had perfection, beautiful fulfillment, and a relationship with the Giver of life.

The words *need* and *want* were not in Eden's dictionary because they could not even imagine anything more. It was what it was, and it was everything!

Then a variable was introduced. Perhaps subtle at first, and then it progressively became stronger and stronger. And now, *they* or *we* only see the one and only thing that we should have to be content. This thought nags at us until nothing we have is enough anymore, or even all that good anymore.

So from the beginning, free will was introduced. Free will is represented by a forbidden fruit. We can make a personal decision about what is right and who we want to follow. Do we believe God or pridefully choose to be our own god and define our own right and wrong? The names and places change, but the story is as old as time.

Without the freedom to choose, we cannot really be free to trust, just obey. And if we cannot choose to trust someone, we cannot really know how to love. We need to be able to love and trust to have relationships that are worth having.

God wanted us to choose to love Him. People can be forced to obey, especially with the right good and bad consequences, but no one can be forced to love. Love is a gift that we give because that love comes from God. He first loved us and gave us the freedom to choose to love Him back. We know this is true because that is the kind of relationship we want with those we love and share life with. Would God not want that kind of love too?

Just think about that in the beginning, there were only two people in this beautiful garden. Keeping up with the neighbors was not a problem for the first family. But Adam and Eve allowed themselves to listen to a thought that caught them off guard. Evil starts with a thought, then the thought takes on a life of its own. It's progressive. Generation after generation seems to become more and more ungrateful. Everyone blames everyone's neighbor for what they deem unfair, and then, blames God.

Eve blamed Adam, Adam blamed Eve, and then it was all God's fault. If God had given them a better wife or husband, if God had not put that one tree right out in the middle where they had to pass it every day, and by the way, the apple that we cannot have is the one thing more that we want. Then we will be satisfied, then we will be content, then we will be in control. Not you, God. We can take it from here.

Yeah, God. It's definitely Your fault. You created the fruit, and You labeled it forbidden. And the one law became ten. And now, the ten laws take up volumes of law books with millions of legalistic words to explain what we can and cannot do. It is all so complicated and has taken on a life of its own. If we would listen to God, we would know all we need to know. But there lies the problem.

We did not want God's *do not*, and now see what we've got… chaos, and more chaos, and more and more chaos beyond anything we could have possibly imagined or certainly wanted.

Now everyone is telling everyone what to do and not do according to what they want to do or not do. The desire to be our own god and decide what is good and what is evil is not working. It's obvious; no one is happy or content for long, and there is no end to the search for something, anything that can fill the emptiness within.

For those who may not know the story, I will include the highlights from Scripture.

> *Now the serpent was the shrewdest of all the*
> *creatures the Lord God had made. "Really?"*
> *he asked the woman. "Did God really say you*
> *must not eat any of the fruit in the garden?"*
> *(Doubt is introduced where*
> *complete trust had been.)*
> *"You won't die!" The serpent hissed. God*
> *knows that your eyes will be opened when*
> *you eat it. You will become just like God,*
> *knowing everything, both good and evil.*
> *(Genesis 3:1–3, The Daily Walk Bible)*

I have studied these verses and know that this is something we all fall for. We are not really told the whole truth but only part of the truth. The serpent came in the form of a snake, but temptation can come in any form, or no form at all. Just an idea, a doubt, a rebellious spirit that tempts us to leave what we know is right and do what we know is wrong.

It's personal to all of us. We all have that line we won't cross, but we do. We all judge others for what we ourselves do but say we do not do. Some are self-righteous, and others want to remove any standard of right or wrong unless, and until, it steps on their own hypocritical shoes. It is like reading today's headlines and seeing the story played out every day and in every generation. It fascinates me and humbles me. I know God is speaking to me.

I was talking to myself as well as the young girls in my Sunday school class. It was like preaching to the choir, and I was sitting in the front row listening to myself and shouting, "Amen!" But inside,

I was quietly trying to reassure myself that God's plan for the future would be better than mine.

So the doubt kept whispering the same old lie, and I had to choose what I believed. And here it is.

I believe in a loving God who has weighed everything carefully. He knows where all the things I cannot know are going. And at the right time, He will reveal how my story will fit perfectly into His finished masterpiece. For I am a valuable strand in His perfect plan.

I was choosing to believe in God's Word and not my feelings. The feelings would have to catch up with the bright future God had waiting for tomorrow's new day. I would turn the corner on the attitude of loss and be thankful for the many promises He had already fulfilled.

After teaching the girls that Sunday when I was experiencing the blessed assurance that God would make everything good in His time, I came down from that spiritual mountaintop to put my faith into practice.

That particular Sunday was another Mother's Day. What I had said, did I really believe? Was this something a Sunday school teacher had told me and life had not given me any reason so far to doubt that it was true, always true? The *groupthink* that works on Sunday, but not so much when God gives us an opportunity to defend what we say we believe. When what we say we believe doesn't line up with the reality that we are personally facing, and our hearts are not feeling the truth found in His Word?

Was I the exception to the beautiful promises of God; the exception and not the rule, the one who is behind the door, and not meant to be invited into the celebration? Well, they would face their own tests and have to find out for themselves because I was not going to rain down doubt on my lesson plan or God's gospel.

Not me. I knew God was able to do anything; He could but had chosen not to give me the baby I wanted. What His purpose was for me I might not know. He wanted to be glorified in my life. How He would do that, I decided to cooperate. To focus on Him and not so much on me. Sounded good, and sounded so spiritual, but I was sure someone else would do it better, one not prone to giant mood swings.

Someone has said that God doesn't call the equipped; He equips the called. That person probably had been tested and knew what he was talking about.

I was continuing to learn from the stories in the Scriptures about how people went through overwhelming obstacles with God's amazing grace. They walked through fiery furnaces, were thrown into hungry lions' dens, were beaten, and suffered every unimaginable evil. This evil was done to destroy the message of His hope in their testimonies, yet their boldness and perseverance are why we remember them today. Their stories give us encouragement and hope for whatever we face.

I was being asked to believe God was good even when I did not have the desire of my heart fulfilled, especially when I knew He could do what He said, and He had said no. And when I asked why, all I heard was silence. He would not even take away the desire to have a child. Must I live with this ache in my heart?

Consider it pure joy, whenever you face trials of many kinds, because you know that the testing of your faith develops perseverance. Perseverance must finish its work so that you may be mature and complete, not lacking anything. (James 1:2–4)

Standing on His Promises

For I am convinced that neither death nor life,
neither angels nor demons, neither the present
nor the future, nor any powers, neither height
nor depth, nor anything else in all creation, will
be able to separate us from the love of God that
is in Christ Jesus our Lord. (Romans 8:38–39)

I am a child of God, standing boldly on His promises. I have closed my eyes to the obstacles and dangers, the impossibilities; and with my life pointed up, took off ever so slowly to my Lord, my Guide, and my Friend.

Did the verses that I learned as a child, those simple verses, only apply to the young and naive? I needed to know. I had been a mediocre Christian long enough. The satisfactory label on my report card, enough to pass to the next grade in elementary school, was not going to define me. Satisfactory was not what I wanted to represent my faith walk with God.

I am an overcomer, I told myself. Like the overcomers in the stories in the Bible, I would come forth as gold, pure gold. That was the child of God I wanted to be. I wanted to be who God said I am, and nothing one iota less.

Yes, I had faith, but how much faith was what I didn't know. I had lots of faith one day and none the next. But God is the one who is the Author of our faith. Even faith is a gift from God, and I wanted more of that gift.

I wanted to be counted among those who were faithful—those who love Him in season and out, in good times and in times of defeat, not a fair-weather fan but a devoted follower, to be all in, not for what He could do to make my life easier or fix what I had broken but for who He is.

So with my fear persistently hanging on, I chose to ignore it and move out in an attitude of expectancy. "Come and see," was the challenge Jesus gave to those who followed Him. I felt Him saying, "Don't look down. Don't look back. Look to Me."

Since I said to my class that nothing is impossible with God, and God had not taken the desire away that I asked for, I cried out in a prayer of desperation. I knew that God did not need my fallopian tubes for me to have a baby. As impossible as that prayer sounded, no matter what was written in my medical file, I believed. I would not go back down the mountain on the ski lift chair of defeat. And just as Jacob wrestled with God until God blessed him, I too would not give up until He blessed me with an answer to my prayer.

And Jacob wrestled with God until he
got his blessing. (Genesis 32:27)

This attitude was not what the enemy expected. I decided that the enemy's power was highly overrated in my life. I had the power to keep the door of my dream open.

So when I asked the Lord, "How big are you?" and when I drew the line in the snow and dared Him to see how He would deal with this highly charged female with the tiniest roar, He did the most amazing thing. An overwhelming assurance came over me. I expected something good.

I surrendered the desire of my heart to Him. If He took the desire away, it was good, and if the desire would always be there, it was good. "Please, dear Lord, do something in my life that only You can do."

And I knew with the assurance of His overwhelming love that I could wait for the whatever.

Was I waiting for a medical science breakthrough or the phone call that moved my name up on the adoption list? I didn't think so. I can't explain what the world would label my irrational feelings, but

I knew the tender sweet voice of my Lord. I would have the baby I prayed for.

A few weeks later, the doctor wanted me to come in for tests. He was confident that there was something wrong. A tumor must be the answer to my symptoms of pregnancy. I was scheduled for a sonogram on Saturday, a day the office normally is closed. I sensed the enemy whispering in my spirit that I had set myself up to be hurt again. The negative side of my emotions was telling me how naive I was again. But I refused to listen. I was not wrong. I would not let a stronghold of doubt take hold of my mind.

> *For though we live in the world, we do not*
> *wage war as the world does. The weapons we*
> *fight with are not the weapons of the world.*
> *On the contrary, they have divine power to*
> *demolish strongholds. (2 Corinthians 10:3–4)*

Our lives reflect our thoughts. And the biggest stronghold that holds us back is the lies we listen to instead of our faith. The truth demolishes the strongholds the enemy tries to get us to believe.

> *We demolish arguments and every pretension*
> *that sets itself up against the knowledge of*
> *God. Take captive every thought to make it*
> *obedient to Christ. (2 Corinthians 10:5)*

Now I was waiting on the doctor as he contemplated the diagnosis and what treatment for the tumor he would recommend. I pushed down the thoughts of...

Would there be a death sentence to bear, and would I lose my hair?

Would he recommend a hysterectomy to a hysterical me?

Is this my cross to bear; this journey of life a continual tangled web between hope and despair?

So in those moments as I waited for the doctor to enter the room, God was speaking in a way that my soul could hear.

Because I was not anxious about anything but had perfect peace. He was guarding my heart and mind. The fertility specialist, Dr. Cameron, who had taken my fallopian tubes out after my tubal pregnancy, opened the door and gave me the news that changed my life forever.

The Tumor

And we know that all things work together for
good, for those who love him and are called
according to his purpose. (Romans 8:28)

"Congratulations, this tumor has a heartbeat!" My doctor now confirmed what I had known. I had asked God to do something that only He could do, and the doctor had to admit that my news defied rational explanation.

But I had the answer: my God was personally involved in my life. I asked Him to do what only He could do. And He did. This miraculous miracle that didn't make rational sense had always been His plan. He knew the desire for this child would far outweigh every obstacle or heartache, and I would not quit wanting and asking for the impossible. And He would use this story so others would know the God I know.

The dream I could not achieve through medical science, God supplied through persistent belief in the unbelievable. I trusted Him through every hope that was removed. I would be blessed with a child, and He would receive the glory and be glorified through my testimony. God does His best work when everything we can understand makes no sense, and the world's answers are not enough.

In the same way that Mary and Martha wanted to know why Jesus kept them waiting until their brother Lazarus had been dead for three days before He came, God waited until everything I had tried to help myself also failed. As He resurrected Lazarus from the dead, He resurrected my dream of being a mother when that dream of ever happening had died. God shed His wonderful grace, His unmerited favor, on me.

Because the Scarlet Thread of His presence runs through the pages of my life.

I Was There…Always There

I was there…
When you demanded to know, did I care,
When you thought I was silent; your question of why?
Over all the years, never satisfied.
I was there…

When the baby promised did not come home,
The sadness you felt when you felt all alone.
A new day, new joy all meaningless to you.
The time would never pass,
Each day…just like the last.

I was there…

When the doctor said to conceive would be an impossibility,
Through all the years of infertility, through
all the years you could not see.
My plan.
I was there. Always there…

Our stories take time to develop. Growing in our faith, our obedience and our commitment takes time. Learning to love and trust God takes time. We are on a journey, and we are getting acquainted with the One who loves us the most and knows what is best.

Never did I imagine that God had so much more than I could see. Not just what I read about, but what He was always doing that I had no clue about. For He is the Waymaker when there is no rational way. He is working on all the rough edges of my character, and someday He will get this rough draft of my life to reflect the image of Christ. But despite my slow progress, I know this is who I am because of Whose I am...

I am a child of God.

I am the righteousness of God through Jesus Christ. I am redeemed.

I am an overcomer.

I am a survivor of every lie formed against me.

I am chosen to have a personal relationship with Jesus. I am loved.

I am blessed beyond measure.

I am a follower of Jesus Christ and enjoy life abundantly. And...

I am a mother. What I always wanted to be...

As I listened to my baby's heartbeat, I wondered who this tiny person was. Who was this little one who had the power to change me and give me a whole new life? Who was the long-awaited answer to my prayers? When God redefined the impossible to bring me such joy.

What a gift you are to me, little one!

We watched the baby's heartbeat on the monitor and waited for the doctor to arrive to put the epidural needle in my back. I was wheeled into the delivery room and moved to a cold table. My marine never intended to go into the delivery room, but at the last moment, he faced his fear, and there he was. He had attended all the birthing classes with me, but when he saw an actual birth in full color on the screen, he decided to sit this one out. So it was quite a surprise to have him there. Both of us felt overwhelmed by this miracle of God that we were able to share.

He was there to see the doctor hold this new life that we had forever anticipated. He was there to see the doctor look at my uterus with complete awe at how I ever conceived. He had no answer. But I knew that God had shown me His favor. The miracle of our son's birth changed our lives forever and our relationship with the One who made that possible, even more.

A Gift from God

The steadfast love of the Lord never ceases,
his mercies never come to an end; they are
new every morning; great is your faithfulness.
(Lamentations 3:22–23 NRSV)

I loved being with child. From the first flutters of life, until they placed him in my arms, it was too unbelievable to express in words.

This baby was one of the most prayed-for in history. Once again, we had seen God's miraculous power as we checked off another answer to prayer at our annual prayer retreat. After waiting for so long, this time the baby shower was for me.

What a party we had, and no one enjoyed their outpouring of love more than me. I was even informed that my mother protected her new grandson to such an extent that no one but her was able to hold him for more than a minute or two. She was counting. In fact, the new grandparents were already anticipating our next ski trip when they could have baby Eric Shawn all to themselves.

We were all in a state of hysteria over our special gift from God, but the one who should get an honorable mention at the very least was my marine, little Eric's dad. The guy who claimed to have had a small part in God's plan was stepping up to take some credit.

This was true, but through all the emotions that preceded this happy day, he was my greatest friend when I needed him the most. On the days when I needed someone to give me a reason to get back up, he supported me and never let me stop believing, even when God removed the last chance of my ever being able to conceive.

We faced everything together. We faced interruptions in our lifestyle, and we faced disappointments too, but to make it easier for me, he never let me see his sadness when I could not conceive.

God gave this wonderful man to me because He knew how much I would need someone with his love and patience, someone who would grow in faith right along with me. We would face the challenges together. But no person can supply all our needs, and to expect that is unfair and also impossible.

Only God can see the future He is preparing for us and knows what we cannot. I chose to love and trust Him no matter what that meant in answer to my prayers, but never did I imagine that God had so much more.

What begins with even the smallest act of faith, in time, turns into His assurance. I have grown in my awareness of His power over all circumstances that threaten my peace. And I know that when I pray, I can move the hands of God.

> *This is the confidence which we have before Him, that if we ask anything according to His will, He hears us. And if we know that He hears us in whatever we ask, we know that we have the requests, which we have asked from Him. (1 John 5:14–15)*

Homecoming

For this child I prayed, and the Lord has
given me the desire of my heart for as long
as he lives, I give him to the Lord.
(1 Samuel 1:27)

Life is a learning process. It has its moments of joy and its times of despair. God, I thought, could have made it easier for me, but then, what would I have learned? I understand that now, now that I'm a parent.

We brought our beautiful son home to banners on the house saying, "Welcome Home, Miracle Baby." The weeks ahead were hectic, with two highly charged parents taking orders from our son on when we could eat and sleep, as we took turns walking the floor and watching our baby breathe.

I became a zombie with little or no sleep while recovering from a cesarean section that made moving around painful. In desperation, I cried out that I didn't have time to be tired and wanted to get rid of the soreness and the pain. Immediately, and I mean immediately, I felt a surge of God's healing power go through me. The soreness and pain disappeared. A coincidence? I don't believe in coincidences; in fact, I am confident that God healed me in a dramatic way. Sometimes prayers take years, and others are immediately answered. Why? I haven't a clue.

No eye has seen, no ear has heard, no mind
has conceived what God has prepared for
those who love him. (1 Corinthians 2:9)

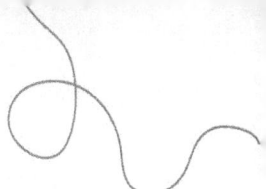

As I said hello to my son, I said goodbye to my father. What an influence this man of God and his prayers have been on my life. He lived only two months after Eric was born, but there was no one prouder of the gift that we had been given. Like Simeon (see Luke 2:25–26) who lived long enough to see the Christ child born and then was ready to leave this world behind to spend eternity with the God he loved and served, my father was ready to return to that place he had seen five years earlier. He had asked us not to pray to keep him here, and this time we let him go.

I will always be grateful that God gave him the opportunity to see the birth of his grandson. God had given him the peace of knowing that my son would fill the void in my mother's life that he would not be there to fill. As I waited in the intensive care unit of the hospital, I thought about the influence he had on my life. He had been the one who prepared me for the future by passing his faith on to me.

My dad's near-death experience was a blow. He went into the hospital for routine gallbladder surgery but came through only to have a heart attack soon after and was given only a few months to live. He tried to recount a vision he saw of Jesus inviting him to heaven. He could choose to come into a place of paradise or to remain. He felt such peace and calm. He didn't want to leave what God had prepared for him.

Then he thought about my mother. He knew she thought she was not able to live without him. My dad had been her life. He loved her and cared for her. He was strong whereas she was weak. He provided for her every need out of his deep love and devotion. His concern was always how to love and protect her, so even though the Lord showed him the breathtaking beauty of the world to come, he chose to stay with my mother.

But that experience changed his life. And the blessing of having him with us for a few more years helped us realize that Dad was waiting for the right time to go. We would have his words to remember: "a beautiful place, more than we could even imagine."

Some might say he was dreaming or hallucinating, but I know my dad, and I know that what he saw was real. It changed him so much that he wanted to be with the God he loved. The God who pulled back the curtain on eternity and showed him things too unbelievably beautiful to put into words...

Oh death, where is your sting?
"In this world you will have sickness, and disease,
trials, persecution, and pain, but take heart,"
Jesus said, "for I have overcome the world."

And as my dad knew, if we have a personal relationship with Jesus, this is not our home, for we are just passing through this life to the next!

That if you confess with your mouth, "Jesus
is Lord," and believe in your heart that God
raised him from the dead, you will be saved.
For it is with your heart that you believe and
are justified, and it is with your mouth that
you confess and are saved. (Romans 10:8–10)

The Life I Always Wanted

Train a child in the way he should go, and when
he is old he shall not turn from it. (Proverbs 22:6)

I was a mom now, and it was harder than I thought. This little boy could care less about how much I had gone through to bring him into the world. He saw little use for hanging on to my hand and following all the good parenting guidelines that were underlined in the book. He was here, he was strong-willed, and he was about to take over. The mischievous look in his eye seemed to imply that he knew how it worked and he could take it from there.

We started out with the highest intentions and soon realized the best of our best-laid plans were best laid back on the shelf. It was like a game of survival of the fittest, and I was definitely handicapped. My challenger was the highly active terminator with a passion for discovering new ways to get me out of the chair and racing across the room before he killed something or damaged something irreplaceable. What was not funny then was my bundle of joy taking a tube of lipstick and drawing the crime scene in red all over the bedspread on its first day on our bed.

The perfect mother had yet to appear. As a new mom, I learned the game of outwitting my opponent with distracting toys or bribes while introducing a new interest to foil the enemy of my sanity. Who was the adult here, you might ask. The book said that I was to be in control, in charge. Yeah, right. He pushed the buttons right on cue, and my typical response was to hop, skip, and jump. An added plus was to hear his name a few decibels above the quiet. But in time, I learned to stand up to this irresistible ball of cuteness and win a few. I loved being my son's mom.

It was quiet now, as I watched him sleep and began to think about those years soon after we brought our baby home. I was a new mom when my dad was in the intensive care unit with only a few short weeks to live. My friends camped out at the house and took care of him so I could be at the hospital.

My mother and I had stepped away from Dad's room for a quick bite to eat when he passed away. We were on our way back to the room, enjoying every precious moment of having Eric in our lives. We felt guilty about not being there, but knowing my father, he probably picked that exact time to leave. We were laughing; life would go on. Eric would fill his place.

I entered a new season of life, a season I experienced through the eyes of my child. The sound of his laughter as we played together was music to my ears. Being a mother was a full-time opportunity, and I loved every minute.

One of the many gifts my son received when he was born was a rabbit that he carried with him for the first five years of his life. Ra Ra was loved and cherished. The love he felt for this ragged and worn-out treasure reminded me of the book *The Velveteen Rabbit*. In this book, a stuffed rabbit became real because he was loved so much.

Many times, we backtracked our day to locate Ra Ra. I remember our mission with flashlights to scope out the territory, beginning with the backyard. Once found, where it had been left unaware, he would fall asleep knowing everything was all right in his world.

These early years were spent learning all about the world he lived in, a world of playing silly games and reading wonderful children's books. There were so many, like *Winnie the Pooh* and the *Tales of Narnia*, that made each day an adventure through the characters on the pages.

One of our favorite books was *The Elves and the Shoemaker*. I would sleep on the couch while Elf Eric busily collected all the shoes he could find and delivered them for the sleeping Shoemaker (my part) to excitedly find in the morning. Or Eric would be the little unsuspecting Billy Goat Gruff who would prance across the bridge only to be frightened by the Troll, who was I, demanding in a deep voice to know who was crossing over his bridge. We even went on safaris with flashlights and discovered dangerous wild stuffed animals hiding in the darkness, unaware.

Every day was summer camp with outings to parks, libraries, museums, or Mother's Day Out. Two days a week we escaped to be with people our own size, and that was good for both of us. I discovered what else was happening in the world; Eric was supposed to learn that he was not the only one in it.

Passing on my faith to him was extremely important. I looked for every teachable moment to instill biblical truths that had been passed on to me. This didn't always result in what I expected, though. For example, Eric loved the popular cartoon *Masters of the Universe*. I didn't want him to believe the popular mindset that He-Man was master of all that God created. Even though it was only make-believe, I wanted to use this moment to help my child learn the truth. I said, "Eric, you know that He-Man is not really master of the universe, don't you?"

I could see the wheels turning in his mind as he excitedly explained, "I know, Mommy. Skeletor is!"

I knew I had to take another approach.

Eric looked forward to the day when he would be big enough to take his lunch box and backpack, climb onto the bus, and ride off to school. I was his playmate until the girls next door came home from school and got off the bus that stopped in front of our house. They played with him when they could, but as they got older, their interest didn't always include him. Then the day finally arrived when he was so excited and proud that he turned five. He would tell them, and they would want to come over and play now that he was big enough.

The next year, he did get on that bus, and it was a day of mixed emotions for me. I was no longer the center of my son's life. I no longer was filling in the teachable moments. I would no longer have a little boy control my entire day when I got up and when I sat down. I had daytime hours all to myself, and now what was I to do?

From the day he climbed onto the big yellow bus, I knew my life would never be the same. My emotions were all over the place again. Yes, I wanted him to be intellectually challenged, but I knew there would be a downside to that also. As the bus pulled away, I was left feeling like roadkill and thinking about everything I forgot to tell him.

In time, I soon discovered there was so much to do that I had little time to feel sorry for myself. I was a room mother and chauffeur. We were on our way to swimming lessons, soccer practice, and Cub Scouts. And it was not a welcomed surprise to learn that we had volunteered to feed and take care of the class tarantula spider and snake over the weekend or during Christmas break.

One thing I enjoyed doing was being a room mother along with other moms who had made the choice to leave the office. Our new occupation, as stay-at-home moms, gave us the opportunity to be in the classroom and help out at school. We planned and supervised class parties, class trips, and whatever we could to keep our children's teachers happy and sane. This personal involvement provided a way for us to know the teachers that influenced our children's lives. An added benefit was knowing the parents of our children's friends.

Those years passed so quickly; the years of big wheels, Legos, transformers, and Matchbox cars. I learned quickly what was *hot* and what was not. For instance, I made the cutest little clown outfit for Halloween and put makeup on his precious little cheeks. He had pompoms on his hat, down the front of his costume, and on his feet. That was the only time that I had any influence over Halloween. Children have their own opinions of what they want to be. Scary is good, but cute is definitely not.

Every holiday was special, but Christmas was the best of all. It was like being a child all over again. One Christmas, we found him asleep under the tree waiting for Santa. He was the best gift for both of us that year. And every birthday brought memories too good to ever forget.

The Pirate Party was one of the best. There was Eric's dad, the big pirate, leading the ten little pirates through the woods behind our house. With a patch over one eye, they looked through the other at the map that would lead them to the treasure. The "X" on the map was finally located by comparing it to the bigger "X" on the ground. When the spot was discovered, the ten overly excited, screaming children took shovels and after several minutes were able to uncover the treasure chest that had been buried many, many centuries before. Mayhem broke out as they took rubber swords in hand and fought to the death.

Then it was back to the safety of the pirate cove to enjoy the cake made by a wrench who had a special talent for making cakes that looked like they came right out of *Treasure Island*. The game of pin the eye patch on the pirate was a big hit too. This prop was furnished by the Daddy Pirate due to the fact that the proverbial donkey just wouldn't do. Then it was off to the presents. Everyone wanted his or her present to be opened first, and it was so hard to decide. In a fit of frenzy, the paper was ripped off and thrown in every direction as I tried my best to teach the manners of thank-you and it's "just what I always wanted." But that would have to wait for another, less hectic day.

We loved everything about parenting. We looked forward to every holiday and every event became special. Birthdays, parades, and trips to the zoo brought out the best in us as we lived through the eyes of a child. Soon, he was able to join us on our annual ski trip to Colorado. Six years old seemed to be a good time to enroll him in bunny school. We planned to go back down the mountain and meet him for lunch but found him at the top of the mountain skiing right behind us. In fact, I felt two little hands on my backside and was surprised to see my little *snow bunny* all the way up to the top of the Colorado Rockies. The ski instructor thought he was so good that he decided to bring him and his little bunny friend up to the top. We saw no need to pay for ski school lessons from that time on. He improved every year, and later we would meet for lunch or at the end of the day. Keeping up with him became too much work. He later became a member of the ski team in high school, and even today, his choice of college was based more on Mt. Mansfield in Vermont than any academic consideration.

His life has been an emotional high for us. What fun it was for us as we cheered him on at all the high school football games we watched him play. I can barely remember my high school prom, but I remember his. I had the picture of him and his first date sitting on the top of my piano. How handsome he looked in the tuxedo that would be returned the next day.

I remember how I felt the day he became the proud owner of a driver's license. That was another day of mixed emotions. I wasn't needed now to sit patiently in the car waiting for him to take piano lessons. Never again would I run out at the last minute frantically searching for a book he needed right away. I didn't need to pick kids up or drop kids off. I had less control over the friends in my child's life, and the teachers who would be taking my place. I was not sure that this was a good thing.

But good thing or not, I would get with the program. The day he eagerly climbed on the bus to go out into the world was an end to one chapter and the beginning of another in our lives. I miss that little boy, I miss the kids running in and out of the house, and I miss the noise and the clutter.

I have the picture of the bus, the pictures of graduation, the prom, the football games he played. I thought about all the wonderful memories we had built over the years. Just think: I almost missed it. If I had listened to what the doctor said instead of believing in what my God could do, those cherished years might never have been part of our lives.

The day we took him to college and dropped him off at his dorm, once again, I was on that roller coaster of emotions. As we drove away from the college dorm that day, I knew he would be challenged to reject everything we believed, and the arguments would sound good. It was more than learning to say please and thank you; we did that very well. He is a thoughtful and giving person, and for that, we can and are so proud.

But the most important, what that really mattered, was passing our faith down to our son—that faith says God is real, and He can be known to those who seek Him; the faith that he will hold on to when he feels alone; a faith that will grow strong in persecution and bring him peace in a world that doesn't know right from wrong; a faith that is his own. And little did I know how many times I would remind myself to give him back to God who loves him even more.

> For this child I prayed, and the Lord has given
> me my request, for as long as I live I will give him
> to the Lord.

Protect him with Your grace, and lead him back to You. Amen.

Family History

What great love the Father has lavished on us, that
we should be called children of God! (1 John 3:1)

When I asked Don, my marine, to add his side of the story to our family history, I was given names and dates, and it was my job to fill in the blanks. So here I go. Don was born in Idaho in 1948. Aberdeen was a small town with a population of about one thousand, including dogs and chickens.

His mom, Peggy, was sixteen when she married Lavoun. He was in the army and returned from the Korean War in 1951. Don's mother was a stay-at-home mom until later when she worked various jobs, such as a waitress in the local café and later in the Simplot potato factory in their town. Ronnie was born five years after Don, and his sister Barbara arrived five years later.

Lavoun started his own business when Don was about five years old. In a few years, he began working in his dad's shop, picking up tools and sweeping floors. As time went on, his responsibilities increased to where he was actually working on cars, fixing damages, and painting them to the customers' satisfaction. Don's dad was also a volunteer fireman and very active in the American Legion.

Life began to change when Don's parents divorced when he was twelve. The kids lived with their dad, and their mom moved to a neighboring town where she worked. A couple of years later, she married Milton. His dad also remarried, and life became very interesting. The new wife had seven kids, and now there were ten; seven were girls. The work included doing lots of dishes, and Don did his fair share. Don was the oldest in this new family and tried his best to keep up with the house chores in addition to working after school at the shop. This marriage lasted three years. Then his dad married his third wife, and his half-brother Terry was born.

During this time, Lavoun opened up a teen club with a soda fountain, snack bar, and pool tables. This provided a place for the kids in town to hang out after school. Don worked there every day until they closed the business. After this marriage also ended in divorce, Don, Ronnie, and Barbara moved back to live with their mom and Milton.

Don had his driver's license at the age of fourteen and began building his own car. It was a 1953 Ford. Then he overhauled and souped up a 1956 Ford Thunderbird engine. Don and his dad began stock car racing these cars on the weekends.

In 1965, he married Wanda when he was sixteen. They were expecting their son, Gordon, who would be born in August. Don worked at the farmers' coop driving a fertilizer truck where he sprayed the crops for the area farmers. The young couple soon divorced in 1967, and Don joined the Marine Corps. He was stationed in Barstow, California, for the first year and a half. Then in 1969, he went to Vietnam and returned in 1970. He was then stationed in Kansas City.

This is where our stories emerged, and I became part of Gordon's life, and he became a wonderful part of mine. On my first visit to Idaho to meet the other members of the family, Don's son was visiting his grandma Peggy. Don took him for a bicycle ride around the town so they could talk. I don't know the details of the conversation, but when they came back, I learned that he had asked him if he could call me Mom.

So that is what I have always been from that day on to this little six-year-old precious boy. We have always shared that kind of love and acceptance. This is an added blessing because families are complicated. But we all seemed to just get along. And even when I needed to teach or correct, he cooperated. It worked.

Once, when Don and I were sitting together on the couch watching TV, Gordon squeezed into the middle of us to sit down.

Now there were plenty of other places he could have chosen, but the message was clear. He liked being with people he loved.

Seems like talkers are more showers in this family because all through the years that I have known my stepson, who dropped the *step* part of our relationship decades ago and has been my son: he has demonstrated his love and acceptance and made room in his life for me, not because he didn't have a loving and thoughtful mother, but because he did, and she, too, has always encouraged him to have others in his life to love and enjoy being with. She was not threatened by that but wanted what was best for her son. Don and Wanda did what was always best for their son.

My friend said I should add something about how Don and I met, and although that was so long ago, I will depend on his memory which has always been better than mine. Details have always been a gift he possessed, and feelings about details have always been what I do better. Together, we filled in each other's blanks. Don and I first met at Eddy's Bar and Grill in Kansas City. It was a blind date, and I was blind because I didn't know I was being set up. He agreed to stop by and take a look because I had a television set. After all, he had just gotten back from Vietnam and hadn't much else to do.

I didn't know I was supposed to meet someone because I was only there to have a fun time with my girlfriend, her boyfriend, and my girlfriend's mom. They all knew lots of people at Eddy's because it was the local neighborhood Cheers. It was their mission to get me out into the real world and away from the isolation and disaster of the last years that were described earlier in this soap opera.

The evening was filled with lots of laughs. We were having the best of times with these returning survivors of war. I remember, almost immediately after Don introduced himself to me, he pulled out a picture of his son, Gordon. He missed him and looked forward to getting back to see him soon. He was stationed in Kansas City at this time, still in the military working for the government in accounting.

As I mentioned in an earlier chapter, Gordon spent time with us in the summers, but after he graduated from high school, he came to live with us in Kansas City. Soon he met and married Brenda, and grandchildren entered our world. They filled in that part of our hearts that needed another child or two. Once again, life was filled with children laughing. The sound of "We love you, Grandma and Grandpa" is like cream on top of the milk, more blessings.

We enjoyed all the quality time, if not quantity time because we moved so much. But we got together as much as possible for summer vacations. Now those grandchildren are grown, and the blessings they bring to us are multiplied a hundredfold.

Although Michele's grandfather, the marine, wore an information technology label and had recently retired as director of IT from the Puma North America Company, and certainly not a minister, our granddaughter wanted her grandfather to facilitate their wedding. Now this was going to be very interesting, I thought. He took this privilege very seriously and worked on what he wanted to say that reflected the vows that came from his heart. The words were perfect, and so was their wedding on that beautiful September day as family and friends watched Jake and Michele pledge their love to each other and their marriage to God.

Soon they took off from Kansas City to spend their honeymoon in Yellowstone National Park. I loved it because that is how we spent our honeymoon fifty years ago. Coincidence? Maybe not, just following in the footsteps of those who have been this way before. They had planned a Northeast trip because Jake had not been out this way before until COVID raised its ugly head, and they went West instead. But two years later, they did drive out to visit us, first stopping in Niagara Falls. It was summer then, and we had their "things they wanted to do" list, and they insisted we must be along. So that was another privilege at our age to spend time with our family, and I have the memories to prove it.

We drove to the Atlantic Ocean and walked along the shoreline of the Marginal Way. We all ate lobster at the Lobster House and shopped in quaint little stores (the shops were on my list). The next day, we went to Boston and took the Freedom Trail Tour of all the historical places in our nation's past. What a great time we had, as we listened to the guide dressed in the attire of Patrick Henry shouting, "Give me liberty or give me death!" Then lunch at the famous Ye Olde Union Oyster House, established in 1826, America's oldest restaurant where George Washington and other patriots frequently ate. It was like stepping back in time to partake of the meal of quail or a pint of ale.

And the time flew by…old people keeping up with the young, but oh… so much fun! By the end of the year, our grandson Michael married the love of his life, Sabrina. Five years later, we have four great-grandchildren: Paisley, Hudson, Sawyer, and Lily. And let me just add…so adorably cute!

These years have been some of the best, but life is not only the high points but also includes the hard ones too. Our granddaughter and Jake have been through four miscarriages during these early years of their lives. I too shared their dream when I was young and faced the reality that what seemed so easy for everyone we knew did not happen for us. "Were children not part of our happiness" seemed to be the message we thought, but like us, they did not give up…

The most heartbreaking time for Michele and Jake came when the doctor could not find their baby's heartbeat which we were all looking forward to hearing at her next appointment. But that did not happen. In the early morning hours, they said goodbye through tears for the baby that they loved. Their loss was so deeply felt by all of us.

Then we were all devastated over the news on Mother's Day when Gordon's wife, Brenda, our lovely daughter-in-love, passed away. We knew she had battled with health issues for a long time, yet it was so unexpected. She was a wonderful, caring person who we all loved and still miss so deeply! And once again, Mother's Day will always be a day they will meet with mixed emotions as I remember so well.

But then, after this sadness, we had the good news that Michele and Jake were expecting again. I began calling friends at church and all over the country to begin praying that this baby would make it all the way to the finish line. Our prayers were answered, and this time they added this precious baby boy to their family along with their two dogs. It was a mixed blessing again after saying goodbye to Sophie, who had spent so many wonderful years with them. They got this puppy when we lived in Kansas City, and what a wonderful companion he had always been. But now, after such a sad year, we had a new beginning.

God brought Kaiden into our world and presented him to the happy couple at the end of November, just in time for Christmas, reminding me that after great sadness, God is not finished. He hears us when we pray. For we were given our son to fill the special place in our hearts that only He could fill, and we named him Eric. I am so thankful for the peace of knowing that God knows what we do not know. How different this could have been because the umbilical cord had been wrapped around Kaiden's head twice and tied in a knot. This was discovered when the doctor decided to do a c-section. God prevented Kaiden from coming through the birth canal. He made sure they got to keep this precious baby boy. He has a plan for his life, and it is going to be oh-so-good!

I thought about how our son Eric came into the world right before my dad passed away to fill the void in our hearts. And now that Brenda is not with us, Kaiden has been added to our family, into that special place that he was meant to fill. Kaiden is filling that place that Eric filled when my dad, like Brenda, moved on to a far, far better place to live. And we too shall see and live with them again. We're part of His family, the family of God.

Life can sure feel like a roller-coaster ride of emotions. There are seasons of joy and seasons of heartache and goodbyes that we don't like and we say aren't fair, but life isn't fair—it's life, and we move on and…

Life goes on, and each day, no matter what, is a day to be thankful for, and I am thankful for each and every one.

I Love Surprises

For My thoughts are not your thoughts, neither
are your ways My ways, saith the Lord. For as
the heavens are higher than the earth, so are My
ways higher than your ways, and My thoughts
higher than yours thoughts. (Isaiah 55:8–9)

I want God to take me higher, deeper, and farther than I can even imagine. I don't want to be satisfied with yesterday's blessings, knowledge, or awareness of His presence, guidance, wisdom, and understanding. I want to begin every morning with a longing for more of Him. Each day, I seek a fresh Word that makes me hunger and thirst for more and more—delicious joy that quenches my senses to the beauty around me as my soul soars higher than the day before.

Those labels of mediocrity, satisfactory, barely enough to pass on with the "better than me peer group" were not going to define me. Whether true or not, that had been the message I thought. But Scripture's message is that He will do more with the one left behind, the one destined not to amount to anything deemed great, or even noticed in the room. He will use any of us if we want to be used. He loves the runt of the litter that the world throws away and gives us whatever we need to be what He created us to be.

I want to soar on wings as an eagle, to run and not grow weary, to walk and not faint. To be planted by the living water and for everything I do to prosper as He promised to those who walk in His truth (Isaiah 43:10, Psalm 1:3). A walking miracle of the change He has made in me, a change in my thinking that I am of little value on the world stage. I know that so many others feel this way too, wondering if their lives matter. We matter to God, and that gives us tremendous value, a priceless treasure to God, to be redeemed at all costs.

When we put each day up against eternity, we have the right perspective on the journey we are on. It is far better to make a difference in the years left and not take one day for granted. When our desire is to know His will and do His will, He transforms the mediocre into faithful followers who love Him with all their hearts, and we love others as He first loved us.

The Scriptures are full of things too wonderful to understand. I love the story in Acts 16, when Paul and Silas felt helpless in their prison cell, doomed, but not for long. While singing praises at midnight, suddenly an earthquake opened the doors and set them free. Surprise, surprise!

In Exodus 2:1–10, we find the amazing story of Moses. He was put in a basket by his mother into the Nile River in a desperate attempt to hide him, then pulled out of the river by the daughter of the evil Pharaoh who wanted him dead, along with all the other babies he had already killed. But she took him home and raised him. He had the best education, and the best military training, and became fully prepared to fulfill God's purpose: freeing the Israelites (his people) from bondage. Surprise, surprise.

God's Word is full of amazing, wonderful surprises. He knows what He is doing, and each life is an important part of His divine plan. When Jesus reveals His gift of salvation to sinners like you and me and turns us into saints through the power of God, that is the greatest surprise of all!

Now I want to live each day with the joy of discovery. A day when the Spirit of God reveals a hidden gem of truth to me, or I receive an answer to a prayer I've prayed for years. His personal intervention made my heart glad. "What are we going to do today, Lord?" I love surprises!

The Bottom Fell Out, Again

A wise woman builds her house; a foolish woman tears hers down with her own hands. Those who follow the right path fear the Lord; those who take the wrong path despise him. (Proverbs 14:1–2)

Everything was fine, thank you, when all of a sudden, the bottom fell out. I had planned to live happily ever after. I had a husband who loved me, a husband who only saw the good in me and ignored all the rest, a husband who never criticized me, always expected the best in me, and always stood his ground in defending me. We never had an argument. We never disagreed, and when I asked, "Do I look fat in this?" he said, "I know the answer to this. No."

"Good answer," I said.

My son had just started middle school when we moved out of the familiar to the great unknown. It was supposed to be a job that was too good to be true, and it was. It appeared to be the perfect answer to a job for him after the old management was replaced by the new.

Like the familiar adage of being seen and not heard did not apply to me as a child, the spiritual truths of God didn't seem to apply. I was facing a midlife crisis. After buying our dream house and living in it for only a few months, it was time to find a new job. The suit company was not selling suits. Leisure was in. But we soon learned that the management had made serious financial mistakes that resulted in them filing for bankruptcy protection. They could not afford the big salaries. It was time to go.

Jesus said, "Simon, Simon, Satan has asked to have all of you, to sift you like wheat. But,

I have pleaded in prayer for you, Simon, that your faith should not fail. So when you have repented and turned to me again, strengthen and build up your brothers." (Luke 22:31–32)

We could replace Simon Peter's name with our own; this applies to all of us who have been sifted like wheat. Like Peter, when persecution and trials come, our faith has failed.

I wish I had recognized the schemes of the enemy and stood firm, depending on God, but instead, I let my emotions take over. Satan knew where to hit me. He knew how to take advantage of me when my focus was on myself.

I allowed a stronghold of discontent to take over my life. The very thing that I loved about my husband Don was his protective nature and his sense of responsibility, and this was the reason why he didn't want to dump all that he was going through on the job on me. He thought he was protecting me. It was not his nature to whine and complain. That was my nature, I was beginning to see.

We are not born spiritual giants; it's something we learn one day at a time. Each day builds on the next. Each trial prepares us for the next. The Lord picks us up, resuscitates us, pumps us up, and sends us back out on the field, saying, "Win the next one for Me. You can do it because I am cheering you on." He is praying for us and pleading our case to the Father. Each encounter with life, and each battle we face teaches us survival skills that strengthen our character, confidence, and commitment.

Trials are going to come. Everything in life is unpredictable and bound to throw us something unexpected. In fact, we can have good times and the struggles of life running parallel. We win some, we lose some, and keep treading life's waters. It's life. God never promised that we would get a pass on the difficult things that hit us. But He did promise He would take us through them and use them for our good.

We grow in the exhilarating feeling of winning over the obstacles that we are meant to overcome through His power. We grow and mature in denying our selfish selves and appreciating God's wisdom and His understanding instead of our own.

Life teaches us through all our experiences so we can pass on what we have hopefully learned and relearned many times. That is what this book is all about: lessons learned in becoming who I was meant to be...

A New Direction

*So be truly glad! There is wonderful joy
ahead, even though the going is rough for a
while down here...You love him even though
you have never seen him; though not seeing
him, you trust him; and even now you are
happy with the inexpressible joy that comes
from heaven itself. (1 Peter 1:6–8 TLB)*

It has been fifteen years since we left that Midwestern town that had been my home all my life. It was exciting, though, to set off in a new direction. It was exciting to see what the Lord was about to do. I was ready for my hopeful future with many blessings.

But the great job opportunity in Ohio went bankrupt a few months after we settled into our dream house in the neighborhood of our choice. Why, I wanted to know, did God allow this to happen? He knew that this company was on the verge of financial disaster, and yet He let us go. Or maybe we were not listening...

Life, at least for me, had become all about me and what I wanted. I needed a lesson on turning it back to God. The verse above says the road is rough for a while down here, and so it is. Job changes, relocations, and other inconveniences are ways He uses to refocus us on what really matters and what really doesn't.

Within a few months, He supplied two new job opportunities that could not have been more different than night and day. We set off for the Northeast.

I didn't want to live in New York; I said that...all the way to New York. We arrived on Gay Pride Day, which was a drastic culture shock. I was not going to be happy and content. I was sure of it. I was sure this was not the best pathway for my life, and we needed to find the exit ramp and get off.

It seemed impossible to find a place to live that met our needs. It seemed impossible to find a house, a school, a church, and a standard of living all in the same place. It seemed hopeless, and I felt helpless. I was very dysfunctional by now. I would like this part to say, "And they lived happily ever after," but that is not the feeling written on my face. No, if God didn't leave the dysfunctional people out of His bestseller, then neither would I, I concluded.

We would not be buying the best house in the neighborhood of our choice, I was beginning to say. We would not find a church that looked like the church we wanted to belong to, I was beginning to say. I was beginning to say that God did not live out here, and neither should I. But I was wrong, surprise, surprise. I am wrong a lot, I was beginning to know.

God needed to put me where I would learn that His ways are not my ways; His thoughts are higher than mine. We had a job. We had to depend on God for all the extras. We would learn to be content with this new inconvenience, and wasn't that the point? Yes.

All the stories I had learned as a child had lessons that needed to be incorporated into my life and attitude. I was learning to trust Him enough to get out of the boat, like Peter, and follow Him when it didn't make sense. I was learning to say, like Esther, "If I perish, I perish." My life was not in danger, but my contentment sure was.

Contentment is not what we have but the choice we make to have an attitude of thankfulness in all things. So like Job, who said that even if God slays me, I will praise Him, I chose to praise Him too, and then things began to change.

We found a house that we loved. We found a school that could not have been a better fit for our son. We found a community that loved us and friends that added so much to our lives. We had it all. We had it all in one place.

Our new church seemed a good fit with wonderful people. Although we had never been Presbyterians before, soon we looked like the rest of them. We were starting a new life in a beautiful area of the country in Basking Ridge, New Jersey.

Don took the train into New York. It was a great job for him, and he loved it. What had started out as a small company soon grew into a large company. God was blessing this company, and we would like to think it was because God was blessing us. This was a modern-day Joseph story. Once I thought coming to the New York area was being sold into slavery, I now saw it as a lesson in humility and an education outside of the Bible belt. We were happy here for many years before God said it was time to move along.

In time, the bigger company that had bought the company wanted to put in their own people. Working for the new owners was very different, and the long hours he was putting in made home life impossible. If God wanted us to go somewhere else, we knew He would do something about it. He did.

The big company gave him his full salary for almost a year when they replaced the old management with new ones. We took the summer off. We took some much-needed vacation. We had dinner together again—in fact, we had twenty-four hours a day together—and now it was time for him to start looking for a job. Not so easy.

It's the over-fifty discrimination thing. It's the salary bracket thing that we knew would be a problem thing. When he was working, he worked enough for two full-time jobs, for an excellent salary. But now, despite his excellent qualifications and background, God gave us a new problem that we needed His help to walk through. And in my journal, I wrote:

"The past is a constant reminder that I am not limited because I am loved and empowered by a limitless God. Look at what You have done for me. The past is my strongest encouragement. My life is a miracle in progress. I have but to pray, and I move the hands of God. You are changing me into the image of what you had in mind, and it begins with my thinking. I think like a victor and not a victim."

I am more than a conqueror. (Romans 8:37)

I am confident. (Psalm 27:13)

*I am confident of this; I will see the
goodness of the Lord in the land of the
living. You are my Shepherd. I shall not
want for any good thing. (Psalm 23)*

*You have made known to me the path of life;
You will fill me with joy in your presence with
eternal pleasures at your right hand. (Psalm 20)*

I am practicing living in Your presence and enjoying every day in a new way. I am listening to You, and abiding in You, and Your words are abiding in me. We're communicating, growing closer, and it took being still, turning off the noise, and expecting You. Like an honored guest that I've invited to come and "sit a spell," we are enjoying each other's company.

I pick up my pen and write because I don't want to forget what You are saying to me as I pray. I want to go back over and over again and read what You are teaching me. Just like Mary in the Bible who sat at Your feet, I too want to worship You, listen to You, and know You.

When the world starts pulling me back and when I fall into old habits of negative thinking, I'll read what we talked about and snap out of it. That's the plan. And I plan to do it again tomorrow.

Filling the Hole

*I am the resurrection and the life. He who
believes in me will live, even though he
dies, and whoever lives and believes in me
will never die. Do you believe this?*

When I was five years old, I remember staying with Mrs. Jones, the lady across the street. Mom and Dad went to my little sister's funeral. She was born with a hole in her heart. My parents tried everything available at the time to save her life, but it was not to be. After about a week, they took off the many tubes on her tiny body, and she went to live with Jesus. They named her Barbara.

I wonder what life would have been like if she had lived. Would we have been best friends as well as sisters? Would we have shared toys and secrets? My brother and sister were much older than me, so I never really felt that I added very much to their lives or happiness. Too spoiled, I'm sure they would say. I did have advantages because there were more advantages at that time. Life was easier for everyone in the 1950s, the beginning of the age of prosperity perhaps, at least for the middle class.

Maybe I would have felt that way if I had to share the spotlight with a newcomer, but I don't think so. I think I would have felt protective and proud of this sister who came to live with me.

I think I know how my mother must have felt. I'm sure she too felt a hole in her heart that time would somehow try to fill. Maybe she blamed herself. It wasn't known at the time that over-the-counter drugs, like aspirins, can affect your unborn child, but that was the sad reality. I know she would have suffered the headaches if she had only known, but she didn't know; no one knew.

The physical hole in Barbara's heart that took her life in some ways resembles the sadness in my heart, that feeling of loss. When the son you love more than life says he used to believe in what he was taught about God, there is a hole and an emptiness that feels like a death. Am I to blame, I wonder?

But I know that faith grows through resistance. God made me a promise that I expect Him to fulfill. "Raise up a child in the way he should go," He said. We did that. I prayed to God and gave our son the foundation to build his faith on. But like so many, the shiny things of life or just wanting to cut the ties that bind them to a belief that never became their own, we, like others, wait and continue to pray they will begin to doubt their doubts in answer to our prayers.

In the Gospel of John 11:25–26, Jesus said to her,

> *I am the resurrection and the life. He who*
> *believes in me will live, even though he*
> *dies, and whoever lives and believes in me*
> *will never die. Do you believe this?*

I believe this, Jesus, but I need our son to believe this too.

> *And when he is old he will not*
> *depart from it. (Proverbs 22:6)*

"Be still and know that I am God," He said to me.

"Be still—not easy for me to do," I replied.

I was confident that God was working in our son's life, and one day he would realize it too and write his own story as I have written mine. I cannot see the answer to the prayers we pray every day, but God is not silent. God fills the hole in my heart with His peace as I trust and rely upon Him.

Dear Lord, there is power in Your name! I call upon all that You are to bless my son with his own faith that draws him to You. I pray that he will one day know You, listen to Your voice, and grow in Your love. I pray that Your favor will follow him all the days of his life and that he will dwell with You forever.

Precious Savior, in the name of Jesus, Amen.

When He has tested me, I will come
forth as gold. (Job 23:10)

A Cord of Three Strands

*Two are better than one because they have a more
satisfying return for their labor; for if either of
them falls, the one will lift up his companion. But
woe to him who is alone when he falls and does not
have another to lift him up. Again, if two lie down
together, then they keep warm; but how can one be
warm alone? And though one can overpower him
who is alone, two can resist him. A cord of three
strands is not quickly broken. (Ecclesiastes 5:9–12)*

February 14, 1971, the card from the man who took me to the ball
said...

"Thirty-three years ago, I asked you to marry me. The future
was unknown, but we had hope and each other, and that was all
that mattered. Now it is February 14, 2004, and the future is still
unknown, but we have hope, and we have each other, and that is all
that matters."

He wrote to me that I could not possibly know how much I
meant to him. He said my love, support, understanding, faithfulness, encouragement, caring example, sense of humor, and our faith
in God for the past thirty-three years continue to give him hope for
our future.

He added:

"I am thankful that we find ourselves in the situation we are
in, for I know that I was destroying the two things that mattered the
most: my relationship with my God and my relationship with my
wife. No matter what life has in store for us, I thank God each day
for you, knowing that I will have inner peace and happiness all the
days of my life because of your love."

I wrote his words in my journal to remind me how God is changing us through these days. One day, when God has put all the pieces of our lives exactly where they truly belong, we will remember our thoughts and feelings and all that we have learned. We learn to be content by experience; there is no other way.

A cord of three strands is not easily broken. For we are united with God and stronger than being alone to face life's challenges.

I wish I could have deserved his praise. I knew that I had failed him so many times. I wanted to be what he thought I was. I was glad that he believed in me. There were so many times that I could have been a better cord, a better wife, a better friend. But he hardly noticed just as God said when others do us wrong, that we do not even notice. That is grace. That is love (see 1 Corinthians 13).

So as I looked at this Valentine's card in my hand, I realized that out of love for me, he did what was hard for him to do: express his feelings. And in the same way, that is why we worship and express our feelings in worship and praise to God, our love to the One who brought us together with Him so our marriage would be strong. Expressing our appreciation to Him and to others is loving Him and loving one another just as He said we should always do.

I pray that out of his glorious riches he may strengthen you with power through His Spirit in your inner being, so that Christ may dwell in your hearts through faith. And I pray that you, being rooted and established in love, may have power, together with all the saints, to grasp how wide and long and high and deep is the love of Christ, and to know this love that surpasses knowledge—that you may be filled to the measure of all the fullness of God. (Ephesians 3:16–19)

Forever Friends

Above all, love each other deeply, because love covers a multitude of sins. Each of you should use whatever gift you have received to serve others, as faithful stewards of God's grace in various forms. (1 Peter 1:4)

Someone has said that if we have one or two friends in our lives who love us, accept us, and are committed to praying for us, then we are truly rich. I am a rich person indeed. It has nothing to do with where we live or what we accumulate but with that feeling that someone values us.

Many people have moved in and out of my life, and I treasure their friendships. Their memories will always hold a special meaning for me. They were there when I needed them most. But as I have expressed, friends move in and out of our lives. It is normal, and we accept change as inevitable. We may not like it, but we accept it just the same.

At this time in my life, I have been blessed with incredibly special friends who have been with me in the "good times" as well as the "not so good."

One special friend is my husband, Don, who has been married to me for the last fifty years, the one who believes in me and always sees the best in me, and my dear friend Karen, whom I have known for the same fifty-plus years. We are prayer partners and have prayed for each other since our days at Sterling Acres, that little Baptist church where we belonged when we were young.

We don't live in the same place anymore. I moved but come back and stay with her often, and she visits wherever I move. I shall never forget Christmas in New York. We rode the train to Penn Station to

see *Beauty and the Beast* on Broadway. We met Don and had dinner after the show. And Karen, her daughter, and her granddaughter came out to visit us on another girls' getaway, driving through the Amish countryside of Pennsylvania, having late-night conversations in hotel rooms, and fun times in Hershey's land of chocolate and amusement park. Now little Mya is all grown up and getting married this summer. We'll be there for her big day for sure.

When I moved to Kentucky, another dear lifetime friend, Suzanne, came out with Karen. Those were happy times and memories that I will cherish forever, especially now that Suzanne has left our trio to be with the Lord. She was a beautiful woman as well as my friend. I miss her and think about her often and all the good times. Even our birthdays were on the same day.

We made more happy memories when Karen and Dick came to visit us in New Jersey. Dick had survived the heart attack years ago but passed away at the end of 2020. The things I remember are things I get to share with my friends. We can laugh even when we grieve. What a man of God with a heart of gold. I can still see him sitting in his chair, working crossword puzzles and reading the latest Clancy or Ted Dekker novel.

Through the years, I have said goodbye to many friends. It goes without saying that the older we are, the statistics are not in our favor. But how we live the days we have left is far more important to me.

I have learned so much from watching my friends live their lives. Their faith in God is awesome! I have watched my husband go through job changes, health crises, and financial devastation and do what he needed to for us. When we had barely enough income due to hospital bills after his stroke, he took on finishing the basement so we would have a place to live. Although we were visitors at New Hampton Community Church, many friends came to help and supplied the workforce that we needed to finish the downstairs. The stroke did not win because God used a man who would not complain and quit when things got tough. And that church where we visited became the place where we have been members serving the Lord for the last ten years.

We all need friends, the right kind of friends who are there for us when we need them the most through the hard knocks in life, for none of us can avoid them. They come.

And Karen is one more example of facing whatever comes her way. She is a breast cancer survivor and is grateful every day. Even losing one of her eyes from a rare complication after cataract surgery and only having limited vision in the other eye is a reason to complain. It isn't part of her nature. Saying goodbye to her lifelong husband and friend may have been the hardest of all. Hard, but her faith is strong. Yes, what a role model to me, and I am so thankful to be her friend.

The people who inspire me are the ones who live closest to God. And when the friends I have known are ready to be taken to their heavenly home, they are ready to go. Their nature is to believe and trust in God, not only when the answers made sense, but when there were no answers that they could know.

How we live our lives is what we get to pass on to the ones we love the most. What will our children and grandchildren think when they remember our lives? Will our family, friends, and the people who witness our lives say that we lived what we believed? What will they learn from our example? Will they find us faithful to the God we say we love and trust?

> *Though John the Baptist never performed*
> *a miraculous sign, all that John said about*
> *this man, (Jesus) was true. And in that place*
> *many believed in Jesus. (John 10:41–42)*

Many believed because of John, the one who, by living his faith, had pointed them to Jesus.

What will my story, the one I leave for those I love, say about me? Did I point them to Jesus? Will the ones I care about, the ones I hope I have influenced in my life, say about me that I lived what I believed?

*Even when I am old and gray, do not
forsake me, O God, till I declare your power
to the next generation, Your might to all
who are to come. (Psalm 71:18 NIV)*

Growing Old

He will wipe every tear from their eyes.
There will be no more death or mourning
or crying or pain, for the old order of things
has passed away. (Revelation 21:4)

I walked into the nursing home looking for my mother. There she was with her handiwork on her lap, making the tiniest stitches. The look of pride on her face over the pillowcases she was embroidering said it all. I remembered how she always enjoyed her hobbies, like crocheting dresser scarves for the furniture or making doll clothes for my dolls. She looked up and began to cry because she was so glad to see me.

We talked about how she was doing, and I could tell that she was making the best of her new living arrangements. She didn't walk very well anymore, and falling was a problem. She talked about the old people who lived there, not seeing herself as one of them. She did like her roommate, and they seemed to have a lot in common. I had prayed that God would bless her with a friend who would appreciate all my mother's good qualities, even her "little bit strange character traits." He sure did. Both women were working on needlework projects and sharing stories about their childhood as if it were only yesterday.

I knew that to her it was only yesterday that my dad had died. She still missed him very much. It had been twenty-three years, but that didn't matter. Then I moved away and took her grandson, and well, the loss must have seemed like death for her again. We talked on the phone, but it's not the same as being there.

Her dear friend Rose died a few years ago. Hours were spent together doing the things they both liked to do. As any teenager can relate to, the time on the phone probably flew by. They were so much alike. How do we replace that kind of friendship? They will always hold their place in our hearts.

I was sending her flowers because I know how much she loves flowers. I sent her candy, especially on special occasions because I know how much she loves a box of chocolates. She would hide them from my sister the same way my son and his grandma would hide them from me. Probably not the best thing for her, but she seldom had candy growing up. It was a way to say, "I love you."

Mother told me how she longed for a doll when she was a little girl that they couldn't afford. "Someone bought it out of the store window," she said, "and she never saw it again." That was so long ago, I thought, and yet she never forgot. Giving my mother gifts was a simple way to help her feel loved and secure—the security she always felt she didn't have, not completely, until my dad.

We talked about her grandson and remembered the day she came to the hospital and looked at him for the first time. We laughed about how she jumped up and down with excitement because she couldn't wait to hold him. We talked about the times he stayed at her house and the walks they took together looking for pretty rocks and turtles.

They spent hours playing games and tricks on each other. They ate the things they wanted when they wanted and as much as they wanted. They had a special relationship. I don't know who was actually the grown-up and who was the child, but it seemed to work.

As I put my arms around her, I told her I loved her and said goodbye. She didn't want to let me go. Growing old, we know, is inevitable. We know we have to accept it. We don't have to like it, and I doubt that any of us do. But these are the memories that we pass on to the ones we love, the memories of a lifetime.

I am beginning to think about old age more than I would like to admit. For example, last year I thought I was dying. It was one thing after another. At first, they were inconveniences, but after a while, I began to see everything as life and death. I convinced myself (with a medical book in hand) that I was terminally ill.

*I cried out to the Lord, and He heard
me and delivered me from all my
anxious fears. (Psalm 34:4)*

Scripture has pulled me out of many a scary place all through my life. In fact, there are 365 references to "do not fear," one for every day of the year, so God does not want us to be anxious about anything. He wants us to pray about everything, and I did and recovered to tackle another battle of the mind another day.

Was I really sick? I sure thought so, and my medical book did too. I traveled to one doctor to fix a problem and then to another to fix the effect of the side effects. Maybe the fear had worn me down and caused all my physical ills, but just the same—they went away when I did what God said. The enemy had me where he wanted me. God stepped in and said enough, and the physical and mental anguish disappeared.

My son would say that I was starting to sound like grandma, who we joke about when she would say she would not be here another year. Well, maybe that was not such a bad thing. He really loved his grandma. Do I feel loved? Oh no, I was sounding insecure.

Treasured Friend

Be devoted to one another in brotherly
love. Honor one another above
yourselves. (Romans 12:10 NIV)

When my friend Karen's husband had a heart attack, I spent the night
with her and her mother, waiting for the crisis to pass. All three of us
were crammed into a tiny room trying to sleep. Of course, we found
that too difficult, not because Dick could be dying, but because we
were laughing. We made a quick trip home to pick up the hot rollers
for her hair. As I remember it now, that was important.

His heart survived, but her mother has since passed away. Such
a fun lady to share Karen with. And when my father had a heart
attack, our friends camped out at the hospital or stayed at the house
to watch our little boy—whatever we needed to make it easier for
me.

I woke up and popped the Foamex pill in my mouth that was
supposed to ward off the ravaging effects of old age when the tele-
phone rang. It's my friend Karen in the Midwest. She needed me to
fix her hair. "It's flat," she said.

"I would love to," I replied, "but not before I've had my coffee."

We are encouraged that no matter what we face that day, whether
it's bad hair or fear and discouragement, we will be okay. Most days
are good to us, while others are not so great. That's life. But if we are
broadsided with bad news or wondering what to do about this or
that, we can take our prayer friend's hand. It's easier that way.

How happy I am that I can walk beside you, lean
on you and live in the warmth of your friendship.
(Winnie the Pooh)

Proud of America

Blessed is the nation whose God is the Lord,
and the people whom He has chosen for his
own inheritance. (Psalm 33:12 KJV)

President Reagan died today, June 5, 2004. I loved him, and so did America. He was a man of character, a role model who made us believe in ourselves. We were proud to be Americans.

He will always be remembered for the fall of communism. He will always be remembered for telling Gorbachev to "tear down this wall." I believe that he united this nation after the Vietnam War, Watergate, and a general sense of pessimism. We were prosperous again. His humor, his optimism, and his faith in God made him the man we respected and admired. He never ran from danger or criticism. He did what was right, and we are a better world for it.

God bless you, Ronald Reagan. Your words are a reminder of how you loved this country and how you believed in the greatness of its people. As you witnessed the horror of the Challenger explosion in space, your words echo in our minds: "They touched the face of God."

Now you too are welcome to enjoy eternity with the God you loved and acknowledged without shame. I know He has prepared a special place for you. You left this one far better because you truly have been America's finest president, for just a time as this. We have loved you, President Ronald Reagan. Rest in perfect peace.

I know in my heart that man is good. That what is right will always eventually triumph. And there's purpose and worth to each and every life. (Ronald Reagan)

Lacking Nothing

Count it all joy, my brothers, when you meet
trials of various kinds, for you know that the
testing of your faith produces steadfastness.
And let steadfastness have its full effect,
that you may be perfect and complete,
lacking in nothing. (James 1:2–4)

We have a job, a wonderful job. God answered our needs. When He was ready to move us to Boston, we were so ready to go. We are in the process of selling that house that we bought in the great neighborhood. Now we are not having much luck selling that house that we were so happy to find. Are we seeing a pattern? So instead of being between jobs at the moment, we are now living in two states at the moment. But this minor inconvenience is just that. We are thankful, taking one day at a time.

As I said earlier, I was born talking. It's what I do best. But this morning, I once again drank my coffee alone. My son left New Jersey yesterday to go back to Vermont to work. My husband left the day before to return to work in Boston. This has been a tough year because we thought we would be unemployed and forced into retirement before we were emotionally ready, but God removed the dark cloud.

And the tough year became a great year. We took a business trip to London. We took a train from Munich to Salzburg, Austria, and enjoyed Mozart's lovely backyard. God knew how much I loved to travel. I inherited this spirit of adventure from my dad, and this job promised the opportunity to do what I always wanted to do. I prayed that next year's business trip would not be to New Jersey. There was talk about Italy or France. I couldn't make up my mind. Oh well, this part of the roller coaster is a good place to be.

But for now, I was alone waiting for the house to sell. I could almost see the marine sitting in the chair across from me. He, too, was drinking his coffee, oblivious to the fact that I had been up for an hour or two and had a few things to say. "Do you ever shut up?" he would say. "You need a girlfriend," he would say. So I thought about that now, now that I was alone, and it made me laugh. If you can laugh even when you are alone, God has made you content.

I have mail, my computer told me. It was a message from Boston. He wanted to know if I would be driving out for the weekend or if he was coming here. His place or mine, he wanted to know.

Someday our lives will resemble normal again. We would live together in the same house, and not in between houses and jobs. We learned to take these inconveniences and frustrations as part of the bigger picture. We were learning and growing in God's favor through each set of circumstances, the good and the hard-to-recognize good.

The doctor said my cholesterol was too high. My Pap test had to be done again because it didn't come back with the right score. I just had a root canal and had to go back. There was an ongoing war in the Middle East. There was always a war in the Middle East. There were brave men and women volunteering to defend our freedom and our way of life. Many would die.

We learn to be content. We learn to be grateful for each and every day. We don't wait for the someday up ahead, the when and ifs of tomorrow. Being content is a choice we make. We choose to fight for the things we believe in. We recognize that we don't always get what we want, but we give it all we've got. Sometimes, we just have to get out of the way. God is full of surprises.

I may not always be happy. Happiness is so dependent on what is happening at the moment, but ah, contentment, that is up to me. Contentment comes by doing what I know is the right thing to do, no matter if anyone else would agree. Contentment is putting the welfare of another before my own without even thinking about it. It's the natural way God intended for us to be.

This is something that takes work. Doing and thinking about others before ourselves is the goal, and it's not natural, it's supernatural, and this is something that I want. To love others is my aim, to trust in the Lord and do good. Wouldn't this be a far, far better world if we all tried to do a little more good?

And being content is knowing God's love and growing in a relationship with Him. And this develops over time as we experience His personal involvement in our lives.

Dear Lord,

When I open my eyes in the morning, Your thoughts are with me. When I close my eyes at night, Your presence is near me.

When I walk about my day or sit quietly, when I laugh, or when I cry, You wrap me in Your loving embrace.

When excited about an accomplishment or something I get to do, I share it with You. Every joy and even pain, emotions high and low, are first sifted through the prism of what purpose for this season must have reason, or You would say no.

For the enemy is crafty and tempts to distract me with shiny things I see. Would I trade so great a legacy and not set the highest priority, and procrastinate the best for something less? Oh, my dear friend, no.

Your supernatural pleasure for this vessel that You treasure. You take delight in me; I can't explain but eagerly claim. For I delight myself in You, my greatest desire to know and live for You.

The Great Commission I Get to Do

Go ye therefore and teach all nations…
teaching them to observe all things whatsoever
I have commanded you: and, lo, I am
with you always, even unto the end of the
world. (Matthew 28:19–20 KJV)

I was honored to be asked to be associate teaching director for Community Bible Study. "Who? Me?" I said. But they sent me to Alabama for training, all expenses paid, because they believed in me. I had such a wonderful time meeting women from all over the nation who would be used by God "to make disciples of Jesus Christ in our communities through caring, in-depth Bible study—available to all."

Talk about feeling accepted, loved, and nurtured—that was me. Then to top it all off, I received a package from the girls back home. Sitting on the bed in the lovely hotel room, I opened every gift and card with the utmost appreciation for their outpouring of support.

How do you measure the worth of your life? It has nothing to do with how much money you make. I don't make any. It doesn't have anything to do with where you live or the house you can afford to buy. That is all in the hands of God. At the end of the day, loving and being loved is all we need, and everything else is extra.

The Message of Reconciliation

*Therefore, if anyone is in Christ, he is a new
creation; the old has gone the new has come. All
this is from God who reconciled us to himself
through Christ and gave us the ministry of
reconciliation: that God was reconciling the world
to himself in Christ not counting men's sins against
them. And He has committed to us the message
of reconciliation. (2 Corinthians 5:17–19)*

Here I am, Lord. I am standing in front of a sanctuary full of women.
Tell me what to say that will make a difference. For the first time in
my life, I wondered if I would open my mouth and nothing would
come out.

My entire life has been about relationships with family and
friends. I was now prepared to talk about my personal relationship
with Jesus. I could hear my daddy saying to me, "Make me proud."

I began this way:

"When my friend Millie calls her daughter Liz before she leaves
a message on the phone, she will say, 'Liz, pick up the phone. It's
your mother.' Liz, if she hears her mother's voice, will pick up the
phone because she knows that someone she loves and someone who
loves her in return is waiting. God wants to have that same kind of
relationship with us. He invites us to pick up the phone and begin a
relationship with Him through His son, Jesus. Christianity is a relationship, a relationship of love.

*For God so loved the world that He gave His only
begotten Son, that whosoever believes in Him shall
not perish but have everlasting life. (John 3:16)*

"At first, it would seem that a verse I have known by heart since I was six years old would be 'a lucky break' for me to talk about, although I believe this verse with all my heart, soul, and mind, explaining it—well, there's the rub.

"How do I explain it so it makes sense to someone who may not have heard it before, even in the United States of America? For those of us who have grown up in Christian homes, we may take the words for granted until we have to fill in twenty or thirty minutes explaining how God so loved the world that He gave His one and only Son. Just think about that. How could God so love this world?

I wasn't around for Pearl Harbor, but it seems like only yesterday that I witnessed September 11. I was at a prayer meeting with the leaders of Community Bible Study when we heard the news. The world is full of hate, prejudice, greed, and envy. Ever since the beginning, when Adam chose to reject God's authority, things haven't been right. "I don't know," I said. "If things are any worse, but they sure aren't any better.

"That He gave His only Son… Now that gets even harder for me. I can somewhat understand unconditional love because I, too, have a child. He's my one and only son. I can understand pretty well about love and sacrifice because I am a parent, but *agape* love? No way. Love my enemies? I really struggle with that, and I call myself a Christian.

"How could God give His one and only Son to die for this world, for the *whosoever*—for you and me?

> He (Jesus) was pierced for our transgressions. He
> was crushed for our iniquities; the punishment
> that brought us peace was laid on Him, and
> by His wounds we are healed. (Isaiah 53:5)

"God so loved. This is the theme of the book of John. In fact, this is the theme from the beginning of time: God's desire to love us and to have us love him in return—a relationship of love."

My audience was smiling—a good sign, I thought. I continued with the chapter in the book of John.

> This is the verdict: Light has come into the
> world, but men loved darkness instead of the
> light because their deeds were evil.

"Now here things get a little easier to comprehend. Good and evil have been the subjects of movies, books, and great works of art and literature."

I heard our youth pastor relate this to the Presbyterians and decided I would give it a try on my captive audience from eleven different denominations.

"You might remember, for instance, that in George Lucas's epic *Star Wars*, things just can't get any darker than near the end of *Return of the Jedi*. Darth Vader and the evil emperor have captured Luke Skywalker. Han Solo, Chewbacca, and Princess Leia are in a trap on the forest moon of Endor. General Calrissian, Admiral Ackbar, and the rebel fleet are fighting a space battle they can't possibly win against impossible odds. It seems like the dark side will be victorious after all. (2003 *Out of Darkness, Into Light*, David Carlton).

"Years earlier, I can remember explaining to my son, who was about five, that He-Man was not Master of the Universe, only to have him look up at me with shocked disbelief and reply, 'I know, Mommy. Skeletor is! There is light, there is dark. They wage a cosmic battle, but neither holds a decisive advantage over the other. In the first century, this was the worldview called dualism. To the mind of a first-century man or woman, dualism made sense: There is light, and there is dark. There is day, and there is night. There is good, and there is bad. There is God. There is the devil. Why else would there be so much pain and suffering? It was almost like two beings of identical power locked in a wrestling match with the world swaying one way or the other depending on who was winning at the moment! And often it seemed like the dark was going to win. Have you felt like that too? We face battles in our own lives. And we wonder: Does God really care, and whose side is He on?"

> *God is light and in Him there is no*
> *darkness at all. (1 John 1:5)*

113

"Let me go on with his analogy. Darkness is merely the absence of light. The two cannot coexist. In the same way, sin, wickedness, evil, and hell itself are all the absence of God. They cannot coexist in God's presence. The good news is that God loved us so much that he sent his Son to be the light in the darkness. When we believe in Him, He removes the darkness and replaces it with His holiness, His goodness, His justice, and love. Through belief in the Son of God, we have been restored to a right relationship with God (*Out of Darkness*). Jesus paid the price for our sin; the debt has been paid."

Whoever believes in him is not condemned,
but whoever does not believe stands
condemned already. (John 1:18)

God so loved that He gave...

I continued, "Let's consider another conversation in literature on this subject between Robinson Crusoe and his pal Friday. Friday wants to know if God is so loving and if God is so powerful, why doesn't He just wipe the devil out and do away with evil? Now that makes sense to me. I can relate to this Friday.

"But God so loved the world that He chose not to. He chose not to do away with the evil dark side. He chose to limit His power for a time. God so loved the world that He gave. He gave us...free will.

"When I think of free will, I think once again of a parent's love. Would I want my son to love me because I gave him life and he had no choice? He had no conscience and could not think or decide. My perfect child could be no other way. It's exciting and I feel so proud when he makes good choices, and I can see him becoming the kind of person I want him to be. Is God so different?

"God knows better than we do that to be able to enjoy a relationship with someone, that person must have the freedom to choose to love you in return. And if God understood that, well, it's pretty black and white. Free will, although it makes evil possible, is the only kind of relationship worth having."

*We are sinners by nature. All have sinned and
fall short of the glory of God. (Romans 3:23)*

*We are sinner by choice. The wages of sin is
death, but the gift of God is eternal life through
Jesus Christ our Lord. (Romans 6:23)*

*Whoever lives by the truth comes
into the light. (John 3:21)*

"Jesus, the Light (John 8:12), reveals for us whether we are of God or not. Now," I said, "God added truth to this picture of salvation. He doesn't get it. Today, we are taught that there is no *absolute truth*. It's kind of like what the meaning of the word is, is…to quote a current event.

"There is your truth and my truth, your good and evil and my good and evil. See how easy this is or how complicated it becomes, depending on all sorts of variables that get thrown into the equation. But this is what God said:"

*I am the Truth, I am the Way, I am the
Life, (the everlasting life) no one comes to
God except through me. (John 14:6)*

"Now we can see why the world loves to live in the dark, why we reject the light—because our deeds are evil. God is just too judgmental, we say, too politically incorrect, we say, too intolerant to suit us…"

*All we like sheep have gone astray; we have
turned to our own way (our own truth), and
the Lord has laid on Him (His one and only
Son) the iniquity of us all. (Isaiah 53:6)*

For God did not send His son into
the world to condemn the world but
to save the world. (John 3:17)

"We condemn ourselves. Remember the free will. Remember, He is holy, and He is light, and they cannot coexist together in the same space. God so loved, and He loved to such a degree that for Him to be truly holy and genuinely loving, He had to be *just*, and He had to be *fair*. We all have the same laws; we all have the same truth. Someone has said that the foot of the cross is level. It makes sense to me. It sounds fair to me. Do you suppose that God knew all along that we would need to find our way back to Him? That if He didn't become flesh and dwell among us to become us so we could become like Him, we would perish? For God became flesh and dwelt among us to save us from our sins."

For the wages of sin is death. But (the good
news is that) the gift of God is eternal life
through Jesus Christ our Lord. (Romans 6:23)

"The Son of God gives us the choice: either we believe in Him and come into the light, or we reject Him and remain in the darkness. No neutral position can be taken. Christianity is a relationship, a relationship with God, the one and only God. Our relationship is personal. It is the relationship of a parent to a child; a Father's love for His children. 'Our Father who art in heaven…' He is personally involved in our lives. And even in death, we shall fear no evil, for our God's love is everlasting.

"I was willing to have God use me. My training in Community Bible Study taught me that He doesn't call the equipped. He equips the called. And God has been preparing me since I was six years old, walking down that church aisle to tell others about all that He had taught me through the years.

"Of course, He could stand on His own. His Words are compelling and speak for themselves. But He decided to use me, not because

I was knowledgeable or good at public speaking, but because I was willing to make Him look good. Just like my daddy, standing me on a table, I was telling them about how good God is. That was the easy part because I knew how good He had been to me.

"Sometimes words will 'cut to the heart and sometimes not. 'Mom, you mean people actually come and listen to what you have to say? You give a lecture, and they listen?'

"My son was home from college. I was now being asked to defend my faith with questions like, 'Did God really say that Jesus is the Son of God?'

"I remembered how the 'intellectuals' at the colleges I attended did their best to deny the existence of God. That question, in one form or another, is asked every day by neighbors, coworkers, and friends who want to know, 'Is God who He says He is, and can He do what He says He can do?' I have asked that question myself. It is for these questions that I study the Word of God. It is then that I can say, 'I know the answer to this!'

"If I knew Hebrew or Greek," I said to my audience, "I would be better equipped from an intellectual side. Since it doesn't make sense to me, I'll stick to something I know. I do understand something about relationships. You see, my mother is in a nursing home, and her health is failing. She never drove a car, so when her grandson was small, she wasn't able to take him to places like libraries and museums. She never went past the sixth grade because of the Depression, so she didn't know much about great works of art or literature.

"But she knew about little boys and what they liked to do. They spent hours together doing stuff little boys like to do. They played tricks on each other and laughed a lot. They ate candy, as much as they wanted, whenever they wanted, even for breakfast. They went on long walks and found box turtles because little boys like box turtles. Eric and his grandmother had a beautiful relationship. They had time for each other, and they spent time together—quality time. Relationships take time.

"Now I know we need balance, and so does God. Parents have to have rules and consequences. We have to see that kids obey and

117

get great SAT scores—grandmothers don't. It's really not fair until we 'get to' be grandparents. Parents represent the 'law,' but Grandma represents 'grace.' I had to help Eric fit into the world, but to Grandma, Eric was her world.

"If you abide in me (spend time with me) and my words abide in you (you know me), ask me for anything, and I will give it to you. For God so loved that He gave us life, abundant life, everlasting life. An everlasting relationship in the Kingdom of God. Thy Kingdom come. Thy will be done on Earth as it is in Heaven. So loved.

"This brings us to the decision we all must make. In Rembrandt's painting *The Return of the Prodigal Son*, we see a son who loved himself so much that he took all that belonged to him and willed to leave. He took his *free will* and left to pursue all that the world had to offer. He willed to leave the Truth, the only Truth, to choose his own truth. And God loves us so much that He lets us go, waiting for us to return.

"Just as the Father waits, we as parents wait for our children to return to the foundations we have laid for them. When they look at our lives, do they know who or what masters our lives? Is it our money, our occupations, or our social commitments that have priority in our lives? If we say that we love God, will they believe that He is truly Master of our world and of our lives? If we so love our children, will we study the Word of God for ourselves so that we can answer their questions when they are small and trusting, and will it last through the pressures they will face? It is far easier to adapt to the opinions of others than to stand your ground in the defense of your faith."

May the favor of the Lord our God rest upon
us; establish the work of our hands for us—yes,
establish the work of our hands. (Psalm 90:17)

"God had a good idea so that all would have the same opportunity for eternal life," I continued.

Whoever believes in the Son has
eternal life. (John 1:36)

"This relationship is not dependent on our income, our social position, our pedigree, heritage, or traditions. It is not dependent on what makes sense, our SAT scores, or our knowledge of great works of literature or art. It doesn't depend on how good or how bad we are because keeping the law is impossible to do. The Old Testament law pointed the way to Jesus just as John the Baptist prepared the way for Jesus, the Passover Lamb of God, who takes away the sins of the world. In the same way that the debt of sin requires a blood sacrifice for the atonement of sins, Jesus, through His death, paid the penalty for our sins. (See Romans 6:23, Genesis 2:17, Proverbs 10:16, Ezekiel 18:4.)

"We have the opportunity to choose to believe and live in the light or remain in the dark. His grace is for you and me; whoever believes has a relationship with the Father through the Son.

"For those who receive Him, to those who believe in His name, He gave the right to become children of God." He gave us the right to be included in the family of God through faith in Him. Christianity is a relationship of love...the greatest love. It doesn't get any better than this!"

I explained how it has always been God's desire for us to know Him, to follow His wise counsel, but most of all, to love Him. He provided through His Son, His one and only Son, the only way to that relationship, knowing even before the world began the debt we could not pay.

Then I closed by inviting them to pick up the phone and begin a personal relationship with God.

I prayed that what I said that day made a difference in their lives. I know the difference His presence has made in mine. It was a wonderful experience and one I felt honored to be given.

And then when I arrived home, there were flowers waiting for me. (He was not to be outdone by the thoughtful deeds of others.) He missed me, he said. Too quiet, I thought, even for him.

Snapshot of Life

Even when I am old and gray, do not
forsake me, O God, till I declare your
power to the next generation, your might
to all who are to come. (Psalm 71:18)

What pictures shall I include in the book I want to write? My mind was flooded with memories as I pick up each one. Some made me laugh, while others brought tears to my eyes from joy as well as remembered pain.

I wondered what happened to the young, size-six woman in the picture that I hold. "This body I now wear is not mine," I said to myself. "I'm sure of it." Photographs show that we have added pounds and subtracted hair. Menopause has raised its ugly head. But despite this fact of life, I found that I was settling into this new chapter of life with grace and contentment on the other side.

I had been working on writing my life experiences, thoughts, and beliefs for the generation to follow, wondering if a book about my struggles and triumphs would actually be interesting or relevant to anyone outside of a few in my captive audience of friends or family—the ones who have been along for the ride.

Maybe not, but God said to write it down, and I had. If someone reads it, and they are encouraged by how God brought me through, then I have made a difference. If they believe that God loves them as much as He loves me and wants to be personally involved in their life, then my life has served a greater purpose. But even if my life has no resemblance to the highs and lows of others, then I wrote these words for no one other than me. I know it was enough for me.

I would like to include only the good stuff—the times of positive thinking and giant leaps of faith, the highs in my life that exclude all the doubts, fears, and hysteria. But how would that help those who need to be encouraged in the middle of their own difficult days? Everything we face helps us to learn and grow. We are better prepared to deal with tomorrow because we have yesterday's struggles to guide our way.

I have discovered that I can pick up a pen and tell God what I think about all these frustrations, all these inconveniences, all these time outs, and it's okay. Because of Jesus, I have that right. I have been given access through Christ into the very presence of God. He is my mediator in the arena of emotions, my ever-present help in times of trouble.

When I start having one of those "why me" pity parties, God brings the good things to mind—the past that He has brought me through with the spoils of war that I was able to claim. I snap out of it every time. It works.

For He knows the path that I take
and when He has tested me, I shall
come forth as gold. (Job 23:10)

Everyone is tested in life. Jesus was led out into the wilderness to be tested. If even Jesus was tested, then why not you and me? Will we stand firm in the midst of our trials? Will we learn from the losses and let God turn them into our gain?

I have always tried to be positive about the things I don't like. "Don't like" is a nice way of saying how I really felt. But God has a far greater purpose than we are able to see, and waiting to see the good is a choice to which I am committed.

I wait for the prayers I have prayed for my children and grandchildren to be answered. I wait for this country that I love to be one nation under God and not the divided one that I see. I wait for relationships that are confined by walls to come down. I wait for the dreams God put in my heart. I wait to see if I will ever get this book finished and if it will make a difference in the lives of the ones I love the most.

I want those I love to know that I have not always been the best wife, mother, friend, or Christian, but I am working on myself with God's help. Hopefully, I pray I will leave a legacy of good.

The expressions of their worth that I wrote in the cards I sent through the years, of how much they meant to me, and that I gave them a view of the God I love that inspired them to want to know Him too. For that would be a life well lived...

The Rhythm of Life's Song

*Wisdom has built her house...the fear of the
Lord is the beginning of wisdom and knowledge
of the Holy One is understanding. For through
me your days will be many, and years will
be added to your life. (Proverbs 9:1, 10)*

Life has a rhythm—a flow to everything under the heavens. There
are seasons that mark out the journey we travel along. Some are the
best times of our lives; then we are smacked down with unexpected
bills, and ills, and what to do about them seems never to end.

Life is like a conductor leading an orchestra. He takes the stick,
and our voices go up high, and then he may hold it there for a long
time before we run out of air and come back down. The baton goes
to the right and then to the left. There are flat notes and sharps as
each note blends into the melody that our one solitary part will fill
in the symphony.

Right now, we're warming up. The instruments are hard to listen to. Too much horn, not enough violin. The drums beat so loud
that we covered our ears. Life's opening is stalled as we practice the
music of the day, preparing for tomorrow.

We have seasons when everything is wonderful and seasons
when things could not look worse, but most of what we experience is
an overlap when the joy is mixed with pain—all bittersweet.

I have been given a life that has many examples of learning from
failures, but I learned from them, and that is what I value most. I
have been blessed with so much, and each day is a brand new one.

I have a son and now a beautiful granddaughter, Payton, that
I was never supposed to have. But science did not know my God. I
continue to pray for our son to know that God loves him and will

one day be walking in the light of truth. College has been a real stumbling block, but I know that God gave this child to me, and his second birth will be even more amazing than the first.

The stroke that my marine had at age sixty-three may have been what the enemy meant for evil, but God meant it for good. He healed him and restored our depleted finances, and now we have finished the construction of the home we had started. I want our family to know that God has always been personally involved in our overcoming the obstacles we have faced. He is the Scarlet Thread that runs through our lives.

We had the wonderful opportunity last year to see our grand-daughter Michele marry Jake, a real asset to our family tree. What a privilege for Don to be asked to facilitate their wedding vows that pledged their love to one another in the sight of God. Don had worked diligently on the message that came from his heart. The tears in his eyes as he recited the words to them were beautiful as they pledged their love to one another.

We have great-grandchildren now. Michael and Sabrina were married the following year and are raising our two great-grandchil-dren, Paisley and Hudson. We will be incredibly old when they marry, but we plan to be here as long as God has a reason to keep us here. We pray that they will raise and teach their children well, and in the way that they should go, and when they are old, they will not depart from it (Proverbs 22:6).

Our son Gordon and his bride Brenda were still getting their mail at the same address after all these years. They were married in our living room and were evidence of the wisdom that love and com-mitment didn't have to start with an expensive wedding. They had weathered the storms of life and handled them with amazing grace. My grandchildren, Michele and Michael, could not have had better parents. They were not spoiled, and that was extremely hard to do in this day and age. But they would be better prepared for the ups and downs ahead.

Moving away from Kansas City was one thing I might have changed if I could. It would be wonderful if our family all lived in the same state. We were miles away, and getting together was limited and expensive. I remember when we moved to Kentucky, the distance to visit was doable, and we planned to do it often. We walked into the Georges' home, and our grandson Michael ran and grabbed my legs and said, "I found you. I found you." I have never forgotten that and how awful it must have been to think people you loved left you.

And this virus had kept us from seeing our son Eric and our granddaughter Payton. We were on lockdown. Christmas was canceled that year, so the presents were waiting until we could be together again. Payton's birthday was coming in a few weeks, and she would be nine. Time was going by faster than I liked, but hopefully, we would all be together again soon.

But Eric didn't get to see his daughter except for the weeks and weekends that were in the court papers. When they had those times together, he was a wonderful father, and she loved her daddy so much. They had quality time together, and Eric was working on getting his quantity time changed. He had an attorney that I had been praying would see the situation and make the outcome come out in his favor. I prayed that she would do what was best for Payton, and what was best for Payton was that her grandparents would be able to spend more time with her too.

I cherished the times we spent together, those first few years. I took her to church when I stayed with her in Vermont when Eric had to work. She always enjoyed going to church with us when she would be visiting us in New Hampshire. She had so much fun with the kids that I taught on Sundays. If I were out of her sight, she would say very loudly, "Where is my grandma?" I hope someday I will be able to take her to Vacation Bible School, and she could go with the kids at church to Camp Berea or Camp Sentinel in the summers. Every time I heard their excitement about all the fun they had, I wanted that for Payton. What I enjoyed as a child, I wanted for my granddaughter too. But whatever time I had, I cherished. She was a gift, a gift that we were never supposed to receive.

We were so happy to hear that Eric got a promotion in his job and a big raise in pay. He had a great work ethic and was responsible just like his dad. He was recognized as a person who cared about others and helped others when they had problems at work, just like his dad. I was so proud of him. I was proud of the kind of father he was to his daughter. It was not easy raising right-side-up children in an upside-down world. They spent time together doing fun things and building memories. Just like we spent time together, and maybe some of what we did together made him a better dad. I would like to think I too had a part to play in making him the good role model he was for Payton to follow.

Eric's dad drove a school bus and enjoyed the extra income in his retirement years. Once again, he had little kids in his day. He missed Payton almost as much as I did. But he had fun with the kids and grandkids of others during the school year. I loved to hear his stories. One made our day when he told us of sliding down an icy hill and coming to an abrupt stop. He asked the children if anyone besides him had wet their pants. This made them giggle.

One that tugged at his heart was on the first day of school. A five-year-old kindergartner ran back to the bus after class and was so glad to see her bus driver. She missed him, she said. To be missed after three hours was a high point of his day.

After having a career in corporate America and making a six-figure salary in New York, Don had never forgotten where he came from. Whether he was at the top of the ladder or driving a bus, he was content. Growing up in a small town in Idaho and now living in a small town in New Hampshire, we were where God wanted us to be.

I was working in home health care. I helped people who could not help themselves. Some needed a companion to share the lonely hours, and others needed the safety that their declining health from dementia required. This too kept a person humble when you did for them what they no longer were able to do for themselves. Each day I was grateful for the health that I had and grateful that I was able to care for others who could not.

It brought me great joy when I could make them laugh and enjoy life a little more.

We enjoyed so many blessings and had another year ahead to look forward to. We would celebrate our fiftieth wedding anniversary that June, and we planned to take a road trip back through the places we used to live on our way to visit family and longtime friends.

As our lives were entering a season where what we had to do was replaced by what we got to do, this was a wonderful place to be. Our family was coming along quite nicely, and we knew we had done a few things right.

We were happily moving along to the rhythm of wisdom's song, and our flat notes seemed somehow to be blending in.

Life's Dance—One Step Forward, Two Steps Back

Christmas Wrap

Yet the Lord longs to be gracious to you;
he rises to show you compassion. For the
Lord is a God of justice. Blessed are all
who wait for him! (Isaiah 30:18 NIV)

My Christmas memories are some of the best. I remember when Eric was small how excited he was to give me a present. He lovingly wrapped the treasure he had made with the most beautiful Christmas wrap he could find. If the paper was too short on one side, not to worry, he would patch it and tape it down. If there was too much on the other end, that too just took more nips and tucks. With enough tape and glue, the treasure inside was somewhat hidden as he excitedly laid it in my lap.

As expected, I would excitedly and tenderly remove all the excess tape that was holding his gift together for me, "Ah, just what I always wanted!" I would gleefully exclaim.

Another great Christmas was the year my stepson Gordon brought the family out to visit. God decided to excite us with a white Christmas that year in New Jersey, which made everything seem magical. We took the train into New York and walked the streets of Fifth Avenue to view the decorated storefronts and watch the skaters at Rockefeller Plaza. The Rockettes performed their dazzling Christmas show at Radio City Music Hall, and we were thoroughly entertained. Even though we could have taken a cruise to the Caribbean for less money, the memories we made were priceless.

That year we had noise once again in the house and clutter everywhere. There was flour in our hair and sugar in our shoes as the grandchildren decorated Christmas cookies in the kitchen. We had sleds riding down our hills and a big, fat snowman in the front yard to boot.

There was laughter at the funny gifts, and everyone was instructed to say when they opened their gifts, "Ah, just what I always wanted."

I did have just what I always wanted. I had a loving husband, was called Mom by two sons, and grandchildren to love and grandchildren who loved me. The relationship I had with all of them was a gift from God. The love we had for each other was a blessing that grew from year to year.

Knowing God's love and His personal involvement in our lives also took time to grow. The more time we spent reading His Word and talking to Him, the more He revealed about Himself. Every day my relationship with God, through Jesus Christ, grew, and I was aware of His presence in my life in so many new and exciting ways.

Relationships take time, and the more time we spend with those we love, the stronger that relationship of love will be.

The Days of Our Lives

*I will repay you for the years the locusts
have eaten… And you will praise the name
of the Lord your God, who has worked
wonders for you. (Joel 2:25–26 NIV)*

Life is full of opportunities to love and share the highs and lows of a person's life. The roller-coaster experiences make us who we are. But most days are neither. Most days are routine. Most days are going through the motions and learning to be content. For example, today was a typical day. I'll explain.

Being stranded at an automobile service center is not a pretty sight. How bored we looked as we sat waiting for our cars to be repaired. It was thoughtful of the management to give us a pot of coffee to drink, but where were the cups? The soap opera that was on the TV didn't seem to be anyone's favorite either. As we watched *Love in the Afternoon*, we let our imaginations take us away from the Goodyear tire store lobby.

One man broke the silence when he made weird noises with his straw at the bottom of his Diet Coke can. How quickly we changed our thought pattern to the best maxi pad for today's active woman and then to the subject of laxatives, which took in a wider audience. The man crunching ice had a good idea to pass the time, but he would be done with that soon.

Every once in a while, a *doctor* would come out to tell someone that their car wouldn't pass the test or for only $99 more, they could have the other hose replaced. We were always being called upon to make these kinds of decisions. We watched people come in; we watched people go out. The hour-and-a-half delay caused most to forget the whole thing and turn around and walk back out after they surveyed our plight.

Driving home, I was gripped with a new sense of freedom. I understood how deeply committed I was to my car. I vowed that I would never again be put through the anguish that I had experienced that day. I was sure that I spoke for the others who had languished for endless hours. Maybe we would meet again someday—but hopefully not in a tire store waiting room.

Most days were similar to the one above—typical. We have one Christmas a year. And for some, that is the worst time of the year. Mother's Days are some of the best for me now, but they haven't always been. Some of us are lucky enough to be blessed with jobs we love, good health, and financial prosperity, but for many, it is a real struggle.

Some days we are wined, dined, and pampered cruising around the southern Caribbean. We are positive that good times are here to stay, and then airplanes fly into the World Trade Center and change our history forever. The battle between good and evil still remains, and the battle to define good and evil is still being fought.

For a while, we forgot our differences. We waved flags. Our leaders sang "God Bless America," and it was a beautiful thing to see. But it is an election year, and we are back to the same old same old. "Nothing new under the sun," as Solomon would say.

In the sixties, there were race riots, and there are race riots in the major cities today. Businesses are looted, and the politicians look the other way. We are in bondage to a mindset that says we must be governed by the powers that be with so many regulations that we can barely breathe. Incremental bondage and the people think that's fine. Freedom is getting harder and harder to find.

Love Your Neighbor

I pray that you, being rooted and established in love, may have power, together with all the saints, to grasp how wide and long and high and deep is the love of Christ, and to know this love that surpasses knowledge—that you may be filled to the measure of all the fullness of God. (Ephesians 3:17–19 NIV)

I have felt God speaking to my heart that He wants me to learn the names of all my neighbors on George Road and pray for them each day. Oh, I know many of you do that already because I was one of your neighbors. Your hearts were hearts of love, compassion, and a "how can I help?"

Friends and neighbors who listened to the promptings of His Spirit, but then, God moved me out of the "everyone thinks like me" zone, and I saw things from a new address, where I was considered an "odd sort of duck" and not from around here from that moment on.

So from the day I first arrived, it seemed there was a new normal, and everyone knew this new normal but me. And the new normal, although not spoken, was that anything after "hello" was too personal.

I want to change that. Instead of a feeling—whether that feeling is right or wrong does not matter as much as the feeling is there—that suggests that if I don't know you, I don't need to know you.

Now this is not the case since I moved farther up north, away from the hustle and bustle of the Boston suburbs to the Norman Rockwell little town of Hebron, New Hampshire. People wave a howdy and there is a big smile added to it, even if they have no clue who you might be.

It seems to be contagious. It's like a virus of good being sent, whether they know who sent it or not. And that is what I am passionate about doing, sending the "I care about you and want you to know why I care about you—His name is Jesus."

When you know Jesus, it's personal. Because He loves you, and it's contagious. It makes you smile, and it makes you want to wave back. It makes you want to know the one who made you smile and the one who made you want to wave back. Then something happens to you when you know that person's name is Jesus. Something begins to change, and that change is compelling. That change, that feeling of wanting to know your neighbor, is a brand-new feeling that you want to do and give away so others will know Him too.

So for those who do not know those around you, I want to ask you to join me in doing what Jesus taught us to do: love our neighbor.

And if your neighbor is meaner than a junkyard dog...well, Jesus loves the neighbor meaner than a junkyard dog, and He wants us to love them and give them a new heart.

I know the love I receive from my little dog Oreo is like the love of Jesus toward me, an unconditional kind of love that is there no matter if I feel neighborly or not, smile back, or say howdy or not. That is the kind of love that changes a junkyard dog into one who will love you with all of their heart—the heart of Jesus.

So once we can get out again and meet and greet our neighbors, let's pray for them and do whatever we can to love them from afar. Then like a virus of good, we will not only wave a howdy, but we will reach out with a great big hug!

And then, as Jesus said, "Come, follow me," because you are not only my neighbor but my friend. Friends know your name, and friends know you when they see you. Friends know your hurts and anxious thoughts. Friends know when you are lost and need someone to help you find your way.

And that, dear friend, is personal!

A Bruised Nation

A Bruised Reed I will not Break,
and a dimly burning wick I will not
extinguish. (Matthew 12:20)

A bruised reed, I believe, represents the spiritual, physical, and weak people. We are a nation full of bruised people. But although our light is losing its fire, Jesus said we can be rekindled.

God has a purpose in all this chaos, and this prophecy of Isaiah, also quoted in Matthew, speaks of Christ's tender, compassionate care for the weak and the downtrodden. That encourages me when I feel weak and downtrodden.

This past year, going on into the next, has pretty much devastated our country, our "the way things ought to look" picture, and it came in a blink of an eye, so to speak. That is a prelude to the way things will be when, in a blink of an eye, the world will be no more.

I am trying to put into practice all that God has been teaching me over a lifetime. How to survive through hardship and persecution of all kinds, even the ones I caused myself.

I accept my weaknesses. I accept and know I am to rejoice in them because I am going to need the tough lessons learned for the days ahead, whatever they bring. God trains and uses everything for good, now or later.

Looking back, it's obvious. People didn't always like me, accept me, and used all manner of evil against me falsely for what I believed or didn't believe. Well, it's going to get worse. Bring it on. Facing my own failures only gives me a new opportunity to relive these things I would so much like to erase. But I get to redo the story I want to tell. I haven't left out the parts that didn't put me in a good light. No, that is the best part because I lived it and learned from it, and I am a survivor. Now I have a story that is worth telling. Even if God is the only one in the audience on opening night, I want His approval. And as His child, He will be proud of the way *we* turned my life around.

God has removed the label I received on my report card in elementary school. The lie that said I am satisfactory and able to pass on to the next grade level, the low expectations, and the runt of the classroom litter. You must pick her, but only after everyone else is chosen. But everyone knows the message clearly. There is a pecking order. The class envy starts early in life, and the struggle to climb up and climb over is never satisfied.

We buy, buy, buy, and do, do, do. We brag and knock down whatever keeps us down, which makes us feel a little better about ourselves for a day. But God's pecking order is that the last shall be first, and the first shall be last. For those who feel weak and wounded, are lifted up and come confidently into His presence to receive abundant love and peace from the heart of God.

That is what I think He means when He talks about us as being a bruised reed that will not break because He will support us and never let us suffer beyond what we can endure. Whatever we go through has a purpose to make us stronger for whatever hits us or comes at us to destroy us, and most of the time, we are unaware, like the year when COVID struck.

When we feel tired of fighting the good fight, we don't quit—we press on. God's Word says we win when we lose. We are rich when we are poor. We are strong when we are weak. Sounds odd to a world that values the wrong claim to fame.

I spend a lot of time thinking about life, the meaning of it all, and how the world sees what is valuable. If I didn't believe in God, how would I look at my life? Probably the same way. You only go around once, and you had better get it. Do it. Take it from the one who has what you want. Get even. Get the rights you deserve. Have it your way.

At the end of the day, would I be happy, content, at peace? I think I would hate life, hate getting out of bed doing the same thing and never getting ahead. When I took out the one in front of me, new obstacles in my way would rob me of the high I expected. And it must be someone's fault, some politician, my lousy parents, or no parents. Excuses that only make you madder and madder and madder still.

So I was thinking. I would still want to believe that good wins over evil and that there is a good that does not change on a dime or when generations come and go. I would believe that God is working all this out for my good and His glory, the things I know about and the things I don't have a clue about.

Last year was a real walk of faith for me and so many others. Yet we sing because this is not the end of the story. There is no better life than knowing the love of Christ and walking daily in His presence. And this is what I know whether I know anything else in this world or not. He can be trusted to know what He is doing, whether we understand what He is doing or not. He is God, and we are not.

I know I am confident that God is not finished with us yet. We may have to live under the heavy hand of an intrusive government, in bondage for years to come, but God never fails. He is not busy with other problems or forgetful. No, He'll do what is right and just. Whether we figure it out or not makes little difference, and in fact, builds our faith in the dark…and it is dark.

This is why I am writing my side of the story. It is my desire that some of you may consider my views on what is going on and pause to consider how I see what is going on.

I became a conservative when I first voted for Ronald Reagan. He loved this country and inspired this nation. The other party hated him and tried to destroy his character in every way they could but to no avail. But the hatred for President Trump was a battle every day trying to get him out of office. They took this country through 24-7 negative news coverage and accused him of doing whatever they could to feed their news cycles, trying to get his supporters to desert him. Well, it didn't work. He stood up to these bullies for this country and for those of us who put him in office. No one else would have taken the constant abuse, and he continues to take it for us. He kept every promise he made to his voters.

But I want you to know why I voted for him and why seventy-four million Trump supporters voted for him. I want you to know that he made us energy-independent for the first time. He stood up for the unborn and put three Supreme Court justices on the court. They believe in upholding the Constitution and the rule of law. He kept his promise to build a wall to keep our borders safe from illegal immigration, sex trafficking, and drugs. He kept his promise and moved the embassy to Jerusalem. Others said they would, but he did it. He brought back manufacturing jobs to this country, gave us the biggest middle-class tax reductions in history, got us out of trade deals that crippled our economy, and created an environment for everyone, especially Black people and Hispanics, to prosper and start their own businesses, creating opportunity zones. He stood up to countries that were taking advantage of us in unfair trade practices.

Countries respected us again instead of using us. They had to pay to defend themselves and not just take our money and our young people to fight in foreign wars. He also got peace treaties in Saudi Arabia. There are so many other examples of all he tirelessly did for this country. He was always working for the American people. But all that good has been destroyed, and it is heartbreaking for me to watch the destruction being done by those who want to remake this country into a Third World country. Those who hate America and teach others to hate America too. We are not a perfect union, but we have done much good in the world. We give more and get persecuted by those who do nothing but take. I know that is how I personally feel.

And the new administration cannot work fast enough to undo all the good that President Trump did in four years. It is like a sickness of hatred. If Trump did it, they cannot let him have credit for anything that was good. But it will be their undoing. God allowed this, and God will vindicate and use it for His purpose. Even now, we see a nation reaping what they have sown with out-of-control energy prices on the rise, the drug cartels getting richer and richer with open borders, rapes, murders, sex trafficking skyrocketing, corruption swept under the rug, and where this will end, nobody knows.

The socialists want to cancel the culture. I lived through the counterculture of the sixties, and I will live through this fiasco too. History does repeat itself. So why not let it go, and this is why. History is being rewritten to lie about everything. Future generations will see everything evil as good and everything good as evil. They have had a lot of practice, I might add. Turn on the TV, and you will hear the schemes they have been working on. They make a charge against the one they have set their sights on, and their charges are what they have been up to themselves and know how it is done. The plan of deception. The old bait-and-switch game of illusion.

Look here and not there because if you were to peek behind the curtain, you would know what is really going on. They have the news media working to keep the sham going. Where has the free press gone? Sold out to become the instrument of whatever false information is needed and as often as needed because who would doubt the most trusted news like CNN? Yeah, right.

I can listen to someone for a short time and know exactly everything I need to know. They spew the talking points on every issue and help spread the opinions, or better said, the propaganda. They know that their listeners trust them because they say they can be trusted, and they know that facts will not be checked. They demonize the other side from ever being heard, and they've gotcha.

The education system has been used to teach you that socialism and communism are good, and the free-market system of capitalism is evil. You will not be permitted to see or know anything counter to that, nor permitted to know all the good this country has done, only the things that were not good, and that will be blown out of proportion to make it appear that what true evil people did was done by all. Karl Marx called the people useful idiots. He was the face of socialism, and his policies were enslaving the American people.

The prosperity you were promised will not materialize for anyone other than the ones in power. They will have the best health care and be able to travel and enjoy the highest quality of life imaginable at your expense. This is just the way it is supposed to work, and you had nothing to compare it with. They made sure of it.

A cancel culture is in the works, and our history is being erased and replaced. From elementary grades through college campuses, hate is being taught to hate this country and its founding fathers as a racist nation. No debate on that is allowed. Only certain people are allowed to speak. They have been discrediting the Bible as myths and superstitions in the universities and interpreting things they know nothing about to keep you from reading it and believing what it says. Just try to be a conservative Christian with a point of view and all hell breaks loose.

Hypocritical at best, but pure evil at the core. Things that are nothing more than indoctrination of the masses will be required reading and glorified, and anyone would believe without question because to do otherwise would mean being ridiculed, ostracized, and probably deemed a nuisance to society and facing harsh penalties and imprisonment for the very things they themselves are doing. Open debate denied.

Election day came without the band playing. Freedom was denied to this country where patriots bled and died to keep us free. This generation has thrown it away for the promises made to give them what they didn't work for by those who did.

The borders are open to all people who want to take. Take your jobs, your health care, your educational opportunities, your savings, and your possessions—just one big happy family. If you work, you pay; if you don't, that's okay.

This government wants the gun rights taken away, no right to assemble, no right to free speech, no rights at all. Just get rid of the Constitution and do what the government wants us to do. Individual rights no more. But they will make it look as if this is good for everyone until you no longer can even think for yourself because that too is against the law.

After all that I have written, know that our trust can never be in a government or its leaders, only in the One who came to set us free from all this dysfunction caused by sin.

Jesus confronted the political powers in His day. He addressed the attitudes that kept people from seeing themselves as sinners in need of a Savior. He exposed the vileness of the human heart that kept people under their control. Freedom...for the human heart longs to be free. And freedom comes from God, and He longs to set us free.

The Brevity of Life

Teach us to realize the brevity of life, so that
we may grow in wisdom. (Psalm 90:12)

What do you do when your life doesn't look like what you had in mind? Well, I don't know, but I do know that I have to find the silver lining in it and glean whatever good can be useful for anyone who likes learning from others' mistakes and not just their own.

What do you do when life seems to change the rules every day and yesterday doesn't apply to what is going on with the attitude of the day? The rude awakening you are faced with is hard to accept, but rude awakening doesn't care.

What can we count on? Like the laws of nature, you know you are on solid ground. Gravity works every time, just like abstinence prevents habits we do not want to continue or pay the debt for. It's the reap-what-you-sow principle that works whether you are a believer or not, or whether you want to live with it or not, and at some point, it comes back and bites us in the you-know-what.

History backs this up. Every story in the Bible backs this up. Our own personal stories back this up. Look around and see example after example from the beginning of time. From Genesis to the world today, eventually good wins and evil gets exposed. Empires come, and empires go. People are up today and forgotten tomorrow. Only a few are truly heroes, while others are remembered as truly evil.

We only have a few days to write our own history. The past has already been written, and tomorrow is what I am working on now. I want to leave a legacy of faith like those who persevered and won.

Teach us to realize the brevity of life, so that
we may grow in wisdom. (Psalm 90:12)

These words of David helped him to end well. God considered him to be a man after His own heart, not perfect, but teachable. He knew he was a sinner in need of God's mercy and cried out to God to create a clean heart and renew a right spirit within him. And we remember him as a hero of faith today. What a legacy he left to us through the Psalms.

Whether it is a nation, a world, or people you may know, perhaps you and me—okay, be honest, you and me. Are we living up to the standard that we had in mind? The world changes the rules on a whim, whenever it pleases. What the world calls good doesn't look good to me.

I fall short of living up to the high standard of God; I don't even live up to my own standards more than I can count. But every day is another day to do it better. I am working on my testimony. I work on being honest and telling the truth. I have stopped expecting to be told the truth by most people, but that does not change who I am.

At one time, the character was like a rule of nature; everyone recognized what it was, and when someone acted dishonestly, selfishly, or disrespectfully, we didn't want to be associated with them. It is the principle of picking your friends wisely—you become what they are.

This generation, more than any time in history, has grown up in a world where parents, teachers, politicians, news media, and whatever role models shape their character, are dishonest, selfish, and disrespectful. It is harder and harder to find those who will do what is right no matter the cost. Opinions are everywhere. But truth is getting impossible to find. And most will not even look.

We live in a society today that has become increasingly hostile. A society that preaches tolerance yet does not look tolerant of anything that does not promote their indoctrination of the new world they are determined to create, not in God's image but their own.

We are a nation addicted to pleasure. The pleasure-of-the-day society is so different from the generation that worked hard from morning to night to put food on the table and was able to survive the Depression and two world wars to secure their nation's freedom.

What one generation would never have accepted, the next makes easier to swallow. Norms are obsolete. What once was common knowledge is anyone's guess. Everyone does what is right in their own eyes, and the bar is anything goes. Children are being groomed to carry it on, exposed to everything imaginable, and their childhoods poisoned by predators and mass media through perverted sex, violence, profanity, and blasphemy. I can't even find a book to read in the library without seeing the f-word used as often as the author thinks people need to hear it. I finally give up and turn it back in.

For the parents who are trying to raise right-side-up kids in an upside-down world, this is an overwhelming battle, but a battle that must be fought—the battle of right and wrong, good and evil.

So I ask the question: What deeply held convictions are we willing to stand on, suffer for, and even die for, as Christians and Jews are doing now more than at any time in history? For me, I want to be among those who counted the cost and willingly pressed on.

This is important. This is the kind of believer I want to be. The person who persevered through all the obstacles life throws to hit, harass, or hurt me with, and passed the test of faith. New norms did not faze me or change the course when the easier way would have been to conform and follow the herd.

The touchy-feely stuff is always changing. If it worked, it would work all the time and not need to be changed. It would be like a natural law. It would not pose the question of why our lives do not look like what we had in mind because life would be in perfect harmony, and look around—it is not.

The world is spiraling out of control. I wonder if others throughout history felt they were the only ones who wondered why. Why they were persecuted for doing what God wanted, some dying without seeing the fruit of their labor, never seeing the ones they prayed for leave their lives of sin and accept the offer of salvation through Jesus?

Cancer is not cured, people reject us, children never come home, broken homes, broken lives, bad leaders, and evil empires gain power. Sin is progressive, it is contagious, and it is not the world that God had in mind when He created it. When He holds it in His hands, what does He think? What went wrong? The perfect world and the perfect future He planned.

What would we do? Throw it away. Baby conceived at the wrong time? Throw it away. Marriage is not exciting compared to the life of everyone else? Throw it away. The nation doesn't supply every want I am entitled to just because I say it is my right? Throw it out. Disrespect those who sacrificed so much to give us the freedom we enjoy and the nation that gave us the opportunity to create our own destinies? Burn it down.

Perhaps every generation feels superior to the last. People want to think they are better if they join this cause or that one, and nothing ever gets better, but it makes them feel better because they tell themselves they care more than everybody else.

This is a pampered generation, an easily offended generation, a bored generation. A generation of victims. This is the constant message they hear, and it keeps them voting for the very same people who keep them victimized. How can people live constantly feeling oppressed and take no personal responsibility for their own lives? Just asking.

I refuse to live blaming others. I am an overcomer. I have overcome a lifetime of getting through one crisis after another, a lifetime of things unfair, a lifetime of things I would certainly not repeat, but I held myself responsible.

An unhappy, ungrateful, hostile society feeds on making others just like them. Misery loves company, and they have plenty of willing converts. Fear seems to be the glue that binds them together. They fear the future, they fear the virus, they fear the people that don't think like they do.

I have chosen not to fear. I discovered that there are 365 verses in the Bible that pertain to not fearing. That is one for every day of the year. One of my favorites is:

Fear not, for I have redeemed you; I have called you by name; you are Mine. (Isaiah 43:1)

God knows my name, and I belong to Him. I can face anything without losing my mind and throwing a fit. I can get up every day and be sure that no matter what happens I am able to survive and thrive.

Now if you are not a believer in God, this promise does not apply. Maybe you did believe, but not now. But did you? Maybe that is the reason you fear the unknown—God wants your fear to turn your heart to Him. And that would be the best thing you could ever do.

This world is our doing. God could have thrown this planet out and created a new one, one less full of *ourselves*, and started anew. But God did not throw us away. He picked up the mess and looked at all the bickering, fighting, destruction, pain, suffering, torn relationships, and the sentence of death that hung around the neck of His creation. He chose to recreate the world, erase all the ugliness of sin and its eternal consequences, and give us a new birth. That is what He has done for me. God is remaking me and writing His redemption story in me that He wants to tell.

These are a few of my thoughts, my deeply held convictions, the things that matter to me, and why they do. They are meant to help you see things through my eyes and for you to know that I am standing up to those who want to shape you into their mold.

My prayers are always with you, even after I am no longer here. Just as my father's prayers and his father's and his grandfather's prayers shaped me, you and your children will be in our prayers. May you always know how much you are loved. Love covers a multitude of all the stuff we wish we had done better or not at all.

I want to be one of the ordinary people who has lived an extraordinary life, to be a part of the stories my children and their children write. One day to have my life reflect what God had in mind—a life worth passing on.

Know My Heart

Search me, O God, and know my heart;
test me and know my anxious thoughts.
See if there is any offensive way in me and lead me
in the way everlasting. (Psalm 139:23–24 NIV)

Thank You, Lord, for this beautiful day. For the rain, for the pain, for the good times or not. I have been given a lot. Help me leave a positive footprint on the lives of others, those who may know me, and those whom I have never met. Forever Yours, Linda.

Relationships come in all sizes. Some are warm and fuzzy; we consider them family, whether they are or we just feel like they belong. And there are those that come in and too quickly move on.

It makes me think: what do others think about the kind of person I am or the person I have become? Did I once fill a need? Was I there for you? Did I do what was best, and did you feel encouraged or discouraged when I left?

This year was passing quickly, and life was going even faster. What have I done to show that I made a positive impression on anyone? Perhaps I'll never know; perhaps you don't know either. Maybe I was a blur on your radar screen. You can't recall my name, but something I did or said has never been forgotten. And it made your heart smile.

For those who know me and those who think they do, maybe your opinion is skewed a bit or could be completely out of whack. Maybe you are all set in your thoughts, made up your mind long ago, and you're comfortable with that. I pray not if it puts me in an unfavorable light. Or maybe someone said something about something I said that may or may not be true. Would you want others to define you?

Now you may love me and overlook a lot, and if that is you, you have given me a gift that I am sure I don't deserve. But why spoil a relationship with too many confessions of all I could or should have done? Those are the things that keep me praying for you without ceasing, and those are the things that keep me humble and my relationship with God closer than ever.

And for those who get thrown into the mix at family gatherings or special occasions, those who did what was expected but would have rather been somewhere else, I feel your pain because I probably caused it.

But you've also caused mine—because I knew you were not where you really wanted to be. But you were there for me. The gift you brought was you, and words cannot express how much that means, how close we were in those early years, but time pulled you away. Never meant to do it, but it happens all the time. A word is misspoken or not meant in that way, and a plank is erected. Not too noticeable, you can see around it and walk around it with no trouble.

Then it may not even be seen at all by the one who said the original offense. Clueless, but damage is done, and the planks get secured into place one at a time until there is a wall that is immovable. Even if relationships are still visible, there is a barrier that is impossible to climb.

Maybe this describes a relationship you have had with a family member or friend. We all tend to get into groupthink. I have been moved around the country from place to place and been exposed to a bunch of people who all think this is the way to think, and no discussion is necessary or tolerated. Yeah, me too.

It is hard to see anything we don't want to see. The shoe on the other foot, so to speak. But I have also been disciplined many times by God, who likes to pull the rug right out from under me when I don't listen to people who are not in the tank with me. Those are humbling experiences that have made me more aware of the human nature that we all share.

Maybe this doesn't apply, and you may wonder what this gibberish is all about. For that, I am grateful. But if our relationship has suffered in any way, and I did nothing to restore what has been lost, then I have lost more than I am willing to pay just to feel right.

And sometimes I was right, but your value I regarded more than saying hurtful things that would build the wall higher. You deserved my respect whether or not we agreed on everything or anything. If you are reading this now, or sometime in the future when I am no longer here, it is in the hands of God. I want you to know.

He reminds me all the time how I did not want to know the things that were so important to my dad until after that chance was gone. I want to believe that he was shown deep in his heart as the person who would one day live by those very things that reflected what he valued most. But I deprived myself of that conversation to share our love for God.

Timely advice is as lovely as golden apples in a silver basket. Valid criticism is as treasured by the one who heeds it as jewelry made from finest gold. (Proverbs 25:11–12)

It is my desire to one day be able to talk about anything with those I love and care about deeply, that we will love and respect each other enough to be comfortable when we don't agree.

I want to listen to you, and understand things from your point of view and hope you will do the same for me. I have compiled a lifetime of my thoughts in these pages and given all who have made it to this page a glimpse of how my beliefs have shaped my thinking and perhaps helped you to see your mom, grandmother, and friend—that is the real me.

I want to apologize for the times I've been wrong. If you want to point them out to me, I'll listen and learn and take to heart what you say and try to see how you see me.

That comes from listening to the wisdom of God, and I learned to listen to God from the example I learned from my dad. And if you remember from the beginning of this story, my dad was a lot like God. At least, that is what he was to me. And that is the legacy I want to pass on to those who never had the chance to meet the one who shaped my growing-up years and the one who was so proud of me.

As I am so proud of all of you.

So Blessed

And Mary said, "My soul magnifies the Lord,
and my spirit rejoices in God my Savior, for he
has looked on the humble estate of his servant.
For behold, from now on all generations
will call me blessed." (Luke 1:46–48)

And for those I am so proud of, I want to talk a little about things that matter—about being moms and being parents in general. These are things that cross my mind when I am still listening to days in the past and what I remember.

We never outgrow being a mom. We outgrow our belief that we will be perfect moms rather quickly. And we are realistic enough to know that we will not raise perfect children rather quickly. If we don't know that our child is not perfect, the world is ready to set us straight. If they are too polite to tell us, we figure it out by the time our child figures out that we are not perfect and they don't want to listen to us anymore. That happens the first time you use the word *no*, and it is all downhill after that. Where did they acquire this mind of their own? I thought we fixed that when we said, "You, child. Me, mother."

From day one, we realize the awesome responsibility we have been given to share in this baby's life. We are definitely not qualified and still trying to get through our own issues, without adding a feeding schedule and sleep disorder. But Mary did raise a perfect child and named him Jesus. She had to ride a mule while nine months pregnant and sleep when she could find a place to lie down out in the wilderness and then give birth to a King in a smelly stable with livestock because there was no room in the inn. But God was with her, in fact in her, and He came into this world in humble surroundings to deliver us from evil. Now just think about how you or I would feel if we had that in our job description. Overwhelmed?

I am supposed to love my neighbor and do good as much as I can, and as often as I can, to as many people as I can. Just like Mother Teresa said in the "Tree of Life" poem on my wall. Well, I am not Mother Teresa, and there are plenty of people who would agree and set me straight. But I try to make a difference, and I bet you do too. In fact, life can sure be superficial if it is not about trying to make a positive difference in someone else's life. The good news is that we get to help and encourage someone who God brings into our lives this very day. Another chance to live justly, show mercy, and walk humbly with our God. That is encouraging in this world, and it is not seen very often. I'm in and willing to give it my best foot forward. God is with me, and I'm praying that He'll do all the talking.

It is the Christmas season when the birth of Jesus takes center stage again. We drove up to the New Hampton Community Church and were greeted by a huge banner that proclaimed, "It's a boy! Jesus Christ, God incarnate, is born today!" I do not want to argue about whether this was the exact date or not because that is not the point. The point is that we celebrate this day when God entered the world in an ordinary way to ordinary people. People who were waiting for the Messiah's birth, and others who thought they had righteousness all figured out and were doing fine all by themselves. And still others who thought they had outgrown their need for Him.

Out of love, He came to show us that we do. He didn't send somebody; He came Himself to testify to the truth that God is real and that God wants to live with us and have a relationship with us. That's personal! God wants to have a personal relationship with me and with you, and that is so overwhelming! But I'm in. How about you?

What a touching scene to watch the little children play their part in the annual Christmas play. Mary and Joseph dressed in robes, slowly walking down the aisle that represented the long road to Bethlehem. Then shepherds, wise men, and angels were added as the baby Jesus was placed in a manger. Pastor Scott read the Christmas story out of the book of Luke, and then there was joyous singing by all. We sang:

"We're coming back to the heart of Christmas 'cause it's all about You, Jesus. We're sorry for the things we've made it, 'cause it's all about You, all about You, Jesus."

Then let the party begin! The cake was brought in with the miniature manger scene adorning the top, plenty of balloons, horns, and party hats to boot! The children of all ages enjoyed the birthday party we had to honor the birth of Jesus. And the reason for the season will be in our hearts forever!

Mother's Day Everyday

Children are a gift from the Lord; they are
a reward from him. (Psalm 127:3)

I am thankful for the little things that are really the biggest things. Those simple, unnoticeable things that so easily are overlooked or never given a second look. But not for me. Every card from my son from the day he was born is kept in the place where everything important is kept.

This year, his Mother's Day card had a place where I easily see the message that he wrote inside that means so much: "I hope this day is special and full of love. To the greatest mom ever."

Hallmark says things like this all the time; it sells, it's business. But the handwritten words that came with the flowers expressed his heart. He has always been thoughtful and never missed a special occasion. Probably more credit is due to his dad.

He hoped it would be special for me and filled with love. I smile and think how special I feel not just on this day, but every day since the day he came into my life, special because God made what others said could never be. Yet here he is, and each day is a reminder of how good God is to me.

There are times I wonder if anyone loves me, if anyone cares. And my feelings just won't let go. Then my eyes see those words that I keep on display, and all the "who cares about me" disappears.

"Encourage someone today" is more than a nice phrase; it's the heart and soul of why we are here and maybe the lifeline to others for which we were chosen.

"To the greatest mom ever." Now that's a stretch. But if being the best means that I never took the gift of his life for granted, then I wear it proudly.

155

Why God chose me to be his mom and not someone else is anyone's guess. To imagine life without the joy of his birth, I could never imagine anything worse.

The card signed, "Love, Eric."

And my heart silently prayed to the One who made his life possible, made it possible for me—the life I always wanted, being a mother and even better…being Eric's mom! For no matter how the world defines me, whether right or wrong, the best part, the who I am, is the one who someday lives up to the words written on that card, the one who leaves a positive footprint on those whom I so dearly love.

Growing in Grace

*For all have sinned and fall short of the
glory of God, and all are justified freely by
his grace through the redemption that came
by Christ Jesus. (Romans 3:23–24)*

A realtor knows if they can get a prospective buyer to see themselves living in the house they are showing, they will make the sale. That is how I want the readers of my story to see themselves in the pages that I lived to tell. For God shed His blessings on me, and even more… His grace.

Grace is His unmerited favor, something we cannot earn; it is a gift. It's a good thing because we all fall short of what God intended when He made us in His image, and we don't come close to looking or sounding like our Creator.

We all have fallen and are even racing to the bottom. We have compromised and convinced ourselves it isn't wrong anymore if we get enough people to agree with you. And that seems to be what is going on from sunup to sundown—getting people to come over to the side you happen to be on, like the game of tug-of-war that we played growing up. There is a line in the sand, whether visible or not, and we hold on to the rope and pull the other side over the line they don't want to cross. That's how we win.

We are judged by how strong we are by being on the right team. By being in the right group, the smarter group, the good group, whether they measure up or not. They line up with those who do. Now this way of hiding our insufficiencies, our *slugger* mentalities, and our guilt, may work for a while, but the game will not last for long. In the quietness of our hearts, we know something isn't right. And that is the voice of God.

Now God's standard is and has always been perfection, so the bar is extremely high. But if we are honest, we don't even live up to our own standards, and that is why we are not content with life even when we get what we think we want. Something new comes out on the market and makes the old not new, and the freedom to do is no longer fun or enough anymore.

This common denominator is that we were never meant to be content without God. We were made in His image and not our own. This rough draft of my life is a condensed version of these struggles, of good and bad consequences, that hopefully give you pause in just doing or not doing the next thing that naturally comes along. For something that seems of little concern when we justify it away will cost more than you or I were ever willing or able to pay. Lost peace, lost contentment, a lost sense of who we really are, and the question, "Is this all there is?" There must be more. And there is…oh, so much more, depending on whose side you are on.

> *I pray that you, being rooted and established*
> *in love, may have power, together with all*
> *the saints, to grasp how wide and long and*
> *high and deep is the love of Christ, and to*
> *know this love that surpasses knowledge—*
> *that you may be filled to the measure of all*
> *the fullness of God. (Ephesians 3:17–18)*

So I hopefully write to more than my captive audience of family and friends who were given a copy and honestly said they would read it. You know who you are. But I also hope others who may pick up a copy enjoy some part or pause before they repeat a foolish decision. If they laugh at my stupidity and not theirs, it is better. If we share in learning from our own mistakes and failures, we can recognize the pitfalls and be better for the next ones that will help us be better mothers, fathers, and friends—whatever relationships that need better relations.

Our lives are still being written. Every day we have a clean sheet to write a better story.

Being happy is a choice that is not dependent on feelings. Sometimes, we are miraculously delivered from the hardship and pain in our lives, but more often, He guides us through them. Then we are able to help others whose lives don't resemble what they had in mind. Our stories have so much more to say. God is speaking. Are we listening?

The unmerited favor of God is a picture of a little child who brings his gift at Christmas to the one who loves him most. I am that child, and I brought my life to God and laid it in His lap—my life with all the tape to cover all the failures and hide the places that I am too ashamed to have Him see.

Pass the nips and tucks to patch what glares at me.

I write… What can I do?
Pride had its grip on me,
Demanding its own way;
Then it led me far away.
What can I do?

My heartfelt cry to You—
The answer came…
To live my life through every frame.
Even when it leads through pain.

For Your glory I shall see.
Jesus, live Your life through me.

For my story is so true,
You live in me and I in You—is what I get to do.

There is no sweeter fame,
Being called by Your Name.

Your child I'll always be…
For all eternity!

> *Oh, child of God, this is what I ask of
> you, to live justly, love mercy, and walk
> humbly with your God. (Micah 6:8)*

Choose Wisely

Then (God) said, "Take now your son, your only
son Isaac, whom you love, and go to the land of
Moriah, and offer him there as a burnt offering
on one of the mountains of which I shall tell
you." Early the next morning Abraham got up
and loaded his donkey. He took with him two of
his servants and his son Isaac. When he had cut
enough wood for the burnt offering, he set out for
the place God had told him about. On the third
day Abraham looked up and saw the place in the
distance. He said to his servants, "Stay here with
the donkey while I and the boy go over there.
We will worship and then we will come back
to you." Abraham took the wood for the burnt
offering and placed it on his son Isaac, and he
himself carried the fire and the knife. As the two
of them went on together, Isaac spoke up and said
to his father Abraham, "Father?" "Yes, my son?"
Abraham replied. "The fire and wood are here,"
Isaac said, "but where is the lamb for the burnt
offering?" Abraham answered, "God himself will
provide the lamb for the burnt offering, my son."
And the two of them went on together. When
they reached the place God had told him about,
Abraham built an altar there and arranged the
wood on it. He bound his son Isaac and laid him
on the altar, on top of the wood. Then he reached
out his hand and took the knife to slay his son.
But the angel of the Lord called out to him from

heaven, "Abraham! Abraham!" "Here I am," he replied. "Do not lay a hand on the boy," he said. "Do not do anything to him. Now I know that you fear God, because you have not withheld from me your son, your only son." (Genesis 22:2–12)

Times of blessing in life are often followed by times of testing.

Has God ever asked you to do something that made no sense—something that seemed to violate everything that you believed about the goodness of God and made you question His love? How could a loving God, whom we trust with what we cherish most, ask us to sacrifice for something that He withholds from our ability to know and understand?

That is what Abraham was asked to do. Abraham and Sarah had prayed for a child, and years went by with Sarah remaining barren. While all around them others were being blessed, they were not. Had God promised them something that He could not deliver? Had they heard wrong, or did they do something wrong—something they had to live with the consequences of, perhaps?

And then when they were well past the probable and into the impossible, God blessed them. Sarah's womb was opened in their later years, in their long past child-bearing years, and Isaac was born. God not only gave them the delight of their heart but also the energy of their youth to enjoy the days ahead with their precious baby boy.

But then, after a short time of enjoying the blessing of Isaac's miraculous birth, witnessing his first steps, hearing his first words, loving, and training that child in the way he should go, they were asked to give him back.

Times of blessing in life are often followed by times of testing.

Why would God give them the blessing of Isaac, the answer to their prayers, and the promise He made to Abraham to make him a father of a great nation, with descendants as numerous as the stars in the heavens, only to then ask the unthinkable—the thing that seemed to violate God's character? Could Abraham still believe in His love?

He faced a crisis of belief, as you and I do when what we believe does not match what we see or know or feel about God. We become confused, and nothing makes sense anymore. Our whole lives are changed forever by what we do next with what we believe or do not believe about God.

Abraham's faith was put on that altar when he obeyed. He believed God had the power over life and death. God used Abraham's faith to build the nation He promised and did not let him follow through in sacrificing his son. Abraham chose to believe when God tested his faith. Was his faith in His Father who loved him or in what He gave him? And the same question is asked of you and me.

Are we tempted to transfer our trust from the One who blesses us with our family, our financial needs, our dream jobs, our good health, or whatever holds first place in our lives—what we cherish and perhaps worship? If we, like Abraham, are asked to go through hard times of persecution and loss, will we stay faithful, pick up our faith, and carry on? Place all we have on the altar of God, knowing that what we see is temporal but what we do not see is ahead...

Abraham saw eternity.

Abraham met the challenge with faith, obedience, and trust in his God. He took God at His Word...

> *By faith Abraham, when he was tested, offered up*
> *Isaac, and he who had received the promise offered*
> *up his only begotten son. (Hebrews 11:8, 12, 17)*

The walk with Isaac carrying the wood where he would be laid on the altar as a sacrifice was more than I can imagine. But Abraham believed even if his son died, yet would he live...someday, maybe not now, but someday after the years or generations passed, he would live again. He knew when God made a promise, He would do what He said He would do.

Abraham told his beloved Isaac that God would provide the sacrifice, and He did when Jesus was born that day in Bethlehem. The promise took two thousand years to be fulfilled, but God never forgot the promise of deliverance by providing the sacrifice for our sins.

Prophets foretold it, but it didn't happen…until the day that Jesus walked up that long hill carrying the cross on which He would die for you and for me. Jesus, carrying His cross, walked the long walk in perfect unity with His Father.

God clothed Himself in human flesh to die in our place so we could live. Our debt is paid, and we will live eternally with Him who conquered the grave for those who trust in Him. His promise made shall be forever kept…

Everything that has been in my past happened to me whether I liked it or not, whether I caused it or not, for a reason. And this reason, which I didn't have a clue about, is coming into focus, and this thread is Jesus—He is the Scarlet Thread that has been personally involved in my days and years and setbacks and tiny steps forward.

Last night, I quietly sat in the little church where our beloved Pastor Scott shared the message of the cross. There were three crosses behind him. Three crosses are empty now, but at one time Jesus hung dying and taking all the punishment meant for me and the ones that hung beside Him. One believed Jesus was who He said, and the other did not.

And the *why* brings the tears once again—the *why* He would do that for me. Who am I? The one who came into this world never meant to be anything special except to the two people who loved me whether or not I ever did anything special and would have loved me no more if I did. To them, I was perfect just the way I am…

And that is how God sees me, the child He chose to bring into this time and place. He gave me fingers and toes and a mind to conceive things He needed me to know. He gave me a passion for all He designed me to do and instructed and guided my course. He equipped me to face each challenge ahead with the gifts and talents that I would need for each day set before me. Like a loving parent, He hugged me close, and then He turned me loose.

I sat quietly before the cross and thanked Him through the tears for the father who taught me about the God he loved and the God whom he loved so much and passed on to his little girl. He took me to the church where I learned to love Him too and trust Him with all my heart. He was my first example of God. He taught me by how he lived, what he said, and what he did, when people were looking and even more when they were not. He passed on more than he could have ever known. His trust in God to lift me up when things were bad and when I could not understand the why or trace His hand; I would hold on to the God he knew because I knew Him too.

And for a mother who taught me to love so many things. I'm sure she never knew. She loved my dad with a God-kind of love, that would sacrifice without expecting anything in return. Her devotion and thankfulness, whether they had much or not, made no difference to her. She developed my gifts and inspired my talents by taking an interest in everything I did. With encouragement and her time and energy, she gave me her love for flower gardens, and when I developed my own, I think of her. She taught me to cook, and messes were expected. I learned to appreciate everything, no matter how tiny and overlooked.

As I later watched her play silly games and walk with her grandson, looking for turtles and pretty rocks, I remembered that the time she spent with me, she was my greatest teacher. These are things I almost forgot, but now God placed them forever in my heart. And I owe her so much more because she gave me her love for children and the desire to have what I would never be and would not give up when told I would never be a mother.

As I sat in the small church listening to the pastor's words, I thought of this son who was never supposed to be born, but he was, and I could not love him more. My prayers for what could never be for me were the plan God had for me all along. The overwhelming gratitude I felt when he was placed in my arms—how God reached down and touched me and made my life so special from that moment on.

I thought of Abraham, and like him, I realized that God builds our faith through testing.

Did you ever pray, and God didn't come when you expected, or do what you expected when you prayed? Days and years go by, and He seems silent. Nothing changes; you are faithful and try to stay hopeful, but nothing happens, and you start believing that what God promised did not apply to you.

Then the happiness you prayed for and longed for comes to be, but it arrives with obstacles you didn't anticipate. Late nights of worry and wondering what you did or didn't do that caused the walls you never meant to build. What you thought would be doesn't look like what you had always imagined. But you will not give up, and you will not stop believing that God will provide. There is so much more than how it looks now, and that someday might be another day or even many years after you are no longer here.

What did Abraham believe? What did he believe about a good and faithful, loving God who would require such a sacrifice? And yet Abraham believed his son's life depended on his complete obedience. Because of Isaac's faith in his father, whom he knew loved him, he followed. He trusted in his father's heart, for he knew how much his father loved him. The angel of the Lord said,

> Do not lay your hand on the lad, or do anything
> to him; for now I know that you fear God, since
> you have not withheld your son, your only son,
> from Me.

Abraham became the father of a great nation; his legacy will last forever through all generations. And we who believe are the seed of Abraham. We are included in the promise.

So as I think of my son, my one and only son, the question remains: Do I trust You, God?

When Eric, my son, my one and only son, was a little boy, I would lie on my back with his tummy on my feet, and we would play airplane. "How big is God, Eric?" And Eric would extend his little legs and arms, balancing high in the air, and squeal, "So big! God is

166

so big!" Then I thought of a camping trip where we were up before the sun.

I said, "We should pray and thank God for the day, Eric."

He looked up into the heavens and yelled as loud as his little voice could, "Good morning, Jesus!" At that very instant, the sky opened up and the sun flooded the gorgeous sky. I remember thinking that in his simple childlike faith, God answered him, just as he expected.

I felt God saying, "Can you trust Me? Can you believe that I will bring him back to that place where he believed in Me and where he laid his faith down?" I knew that I had to let him go. I had to give my son to the God who loves him and defied rational explanations to bring him into this world and into my heart.

Even if I never see that day, I will believe. For without God, like Abraham, there would be no Isaac, and there would be no Eric, and God is not finished with our story.

> God whispers to us in our pleasure, speaks to us
> in our conscience but shouts to us in our pain.
> (C. S. Lewis)

Boundary Lines Are Good

*Now we can come fearlessly right into
God's presence, assured of his glad welcome
when we come with Christ and trust
in him. (Ephesians 3:12 TLB)*

Who can know You, God? Who can understand this vast plan? Is it possible to see? And then, the gentle whisper to my heart, the voice so clear upon my ear: Nothing can be kept from Me; I see; I know. From the beginning of history—your history, not Mine—for I had no beginning...I AM.

Boundary lines keep people and nations safe, but humanity has continually worked to tear them down, creating their own good, God's protection thrown away. The world progressed into a scary place, a mean and nasty place, a place that worships what God made instead of God, the Creator of all things. Do we actually believe that we possess the power to save or destroy this planet?

I love how God answers this arrogance in Job (38:1–41:34). I wrote in the margin of my Bible, "Hey, Job, do you think you are big enough to pick a fight with me?"

God asks Job a series of questions that were impossible for Job to answer. Job was humbled and recognized that God is in control and knows what He is doing or allowing, especially when we are going through personal tragedies, like Job.

When God created everything that was made, He said it was good, very, very good. He gave us a good conscience, and we trashed it. Doing things that once we were ashamed of, but now, do so blatantly; we decided to let our conscience be our guide. God knows we don't use the one we've got. We were created in His image, and He

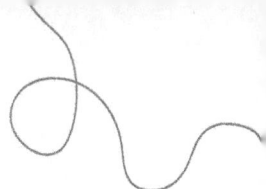

doesn't like what He sees. And if we are honest, we don't like what we see either. As He said in His Word,

> *I Am God and there is no other. I Am God*
> *there is no other God but me. I know the*
> *end from the beginning, from everlasting*
> *to everlasting, I Am God. Who can say*
> *what have you done. (Isaiah 46:10)*

I paraphrase it something like this…

"Well, I am done. I have allowed all this destruction, all these wars to take place and escalate, your enemies to take you over, and remove the freedom you misused. Now you will be slaves in your own land. So don't cry for help, I will not listen. You didn't need Me, America, or acknowledge Me. Goodbye!"

These are my thoughts. I am writing about this so those in the future will know my personal beliefs on the current news of the day.

A nation divided cannot stand. It's a fact, a principle written in Scripture; it's provable, every time, like the laws of nature. God also said, "You reap what you sow." And our nation has sown, and now, reaps a whirlwind. What goes around comes around. Hate too. This country spews forth a bitter, hostile spirit not against its own enemy but toward each other. There are people who would rather see the country destroyed than do what's best for America. And we are getting paid big losses for this bitter, angry root that we have fed continually through the airwaves of our country.

The seeds of progressive hate have been planted in the rich soil of our children's minds. And they are not a happy and content generation as they take to the streets. Elections have consequences. Each generation of liberal, radical thinking believes their own goodness will fix it later when the dust settles. There are hearings in Congress over this, but nothing will change.

The universities should be places where young people are taught to think, but they are not anymore. Socialism and communism are taught without history's evil impact. Anti-Semitic hatred is tolerated and accepted today by an alarming number. This is scary.

We have never been more divided. The fires have been stoked to blaze away. Two Americas exist. A nation cannot stand forsaking its Maker. And we are so divided over God, who created us and allowed us to even become a nation. If one good thing can come out of our throwing away our liberty for the tyranny of government control, it is that this bondage will force us to come together and be one nation under God and fight for what God says is good. Because it works.

Where there is confusion, there is disorder, and we all fail and destroy our nation. And without God, we destroy our very souls. God's good sees no White versus Black America, no young against old, no male and female against each other, rich or poor, but everyone working for what is best for all of America. We will work together to make this country strong. Drop the labels and be Americans.

Who will fix us? Will we rally around a deliverer? God's people came together around Moses, Abraham, and Esther, and the nation of Israel was saved. And George Washington, Abe Lincoln, Churchill, Margaret Thatcher, and President Reagan, I regard as heroes on the world stage. We are a stiff-necked people being led away into bondage rather than calling out to God to deliver us from the evil in our own human hearts. Freedom is only one generation away from being lost. Perhaps God will come and save us.

> *If My people who are called by My name will*
> *humble themselves and pray and turn from their*
> *wicked ways, I will hear from heaven and forgive*
> *their sins and heal their land. (2 Chronicles 7:14)*

God has promised that if we seek His face, He will rescue us and we will be His people, and He will be our God. This is the legacy that I pray my children and their children will be able to have—not living in bondage, but free...truly free!

Jesus Told Stories

How great is the love the Father has lavished
on us, that we should be called children of
God! And that is what we are! (1 John 3:1)

Jesus told stories. We all love stories. We might not hear much of what someone is saying, but when you hear, "I knew a guy once who did this or that" or "Let me tell you about what happened the other day," our ears perk up and our body comes to attention. We focus.

Jesus knew how to tell a good story. Some make us shake our heads in agreement. We can see the punchline coming because we all have been there, done that, and got the T-shirt to prove the lesson we learned the hard way.

Now if you didn't grow up going to Sunday school and hearing these stories, you may not know anything about Daniel and the lion's den, David slaying the giant, Esther and the evil plot against her people, Peter walking on water, Jesus calming the sea, and the many other miracles he performed.

Perhaps Hollywood or culture has put their own spin on them as they are prone to do. Or what you may have heard may be another version of the actual takeaway lesson that Jesus taught. The story is teaching a principle, and this principle is saying something that Jesus thought was important. So important that in a busy schedule, He sat down in the middle of the day and welcomed all the little children to come and listen.

And as recorded in Scripture, this ticked off the disciples, who thought like the general public that children had little value. But Jesus rebuked them and said that these children's hearts were eager to listen and learn what he was teaching them, and such is the kingdom of God. Their value was far more precious than the general public could even comprehend.

The children understood that their Teacher loved them, their Teacher had time for them, and their Teacher listened to them. They loved Him and wanted to be with Him and hear His stories.

Jesus was teaching by example that every life matters. Every life, rich or poor, slave or free, male or female, and children of all ages, are welcome in the Kingdom of God when they hear about His love and belief.

His teachings were meant to make us think, and His teachings created word pictures so that we could understand. Then we would not want to do the things that are wrong but do the things that are right. We would want to be like our Teacher who knew how to tell a good story, so our story would be a good story to tell.

> *At that time Jesus, full of joy through the Holy Spirit, said, "I praise you, Father, Lord of heaven and earth, because you have hidden these things from the wise and learned and revealed them to little children. Yes, Father, for this was your good pleasure." (Luke 21)*

This is what I want to be. I want to be teachable; I want to listen to be wise. I do not want to be like the Pharisees, who were the muckety-mucks of their day, thinking they knew better than anyone else, or the disciples, who thought Jesus was too important to waste his time on a little child.

I think about this on Sundays when I teach little children. I also reflect on the years I taught women of all ages in community Bible study. I have learned rather quickly that the more I learn, the more I want to learn, and that my hunger to know more is never satisfied. I remember my son, like kids in general, loved playing video games. There are levels that lead to new levels, which are challenging and exciting.

That is the same for me. The more I dig into God's Word, the more I discover, and the more I just have to see the next thing God wants me to see. There are verses, passages, and stories that I have read, and thought I knew exactly what they were saying. Then all of a sudden, my mind gets hit like a bolt of lightning from above, and what I thought I knew was only what I could see on the surface. God opens up a deeper level and delights me with something only He could show me and how it applies to me. That is exciting, and I want it to be exciting for children whether they are seven or eighty-seven.

What I learned as a child has been tested, and it is so true. God gives us just enough to whet our appetite so we will seek Him. When we think we know it all, have heard it all, and try to pass it all on, we learn rather quickly that a little five-year-old can teach us something wiser than we ever thought or knew. That is humbling, and that makes us teachable. That is having a heart like the heart of a child.

And we learn rather quickly that we know so little. For all of us, no matter the age or depth of our Bible knowledge, we come as little children, for as Jesus said to all, such is the kingdom of God.

Promise Keeper

*I will repay you for the years the locust
have eaten. And you will praise the name
of the Lord your God, who has worked
wonders for you. (Joel 2:25–26)*

You, Lord, keep Your promises to a thousand generations, and I am not an exception to Your Word! Satan will not have this family, Satan will not have our future, and Satan will not have our faith. In fact, we are taking back everything he has tried to rob, steal, and destroy. His purpose is to weaken me with lies and plague me with the "who do you think you are?" question. But my identity is secure, for I know I am a redeemed child of the Living God.

You are my light in the darkness. You would have to fail when I am trusting You, for me to fail. Your presence is my compass that says, "This is the way, walk in it." The right choice is illuminated, drawing me to the place I needed to be that You prepared for me before my life began. Even when the journey is dark and dangerous, Your hand guides me, for You see what I cannot, the eternal prize set before me.

When I am easily distracted, there You are, my faithful Friend. When the glittery things of the world threaten to draw me away, Your presence within reminds me to remain firm and steadfast in what has true and lasting value. The longing of my heart is satisfied in what You alone want for me because You are the Scarlet Thread that is woven into my DNA.

I know who I am; I will not be shaken. I will be aware of traps set up against my identity. I will not be held captive to the world's thinking. What sounds too good to be true usually is a bait-and-switch tactic that becomes a thought, then a habit of negativity, and brick by brick we forget the blessings and the benefits that our identity with Christ provides. I know it well; I am a recovering "dupe" for the Enemy. He may put the thought in our minds, but we choose to give birth to it.

Dr. Carolyn Leaf says it this way: our thoughts "occupy mental 'real estate.' Thoughts are active; they grow and change. Every time you have a thought, it is actively changing your brain and your body—for better or worse."

And who couldn't use a better brain and body? Changing our attitudes is a good place to start. When we reconnect to what God wants for us and what He wants to do through us, He will breathe life back into the depleted and dead places. He will restore what the enemy has taken from us and from our family's future.

As written in Psalm 107:43,

> *Those who are wise will take all this to heart; they*
> *will see in our history the faithful love of the Lord.*

That is what I want my story to reveal—a history of faithful love to my Lord to pass down to my family. I am writing the legacy I want them to read that says why it matters so much to me. That we will be His people, and He will be our God.

Father God, I dedicate our children and grandchildren to You and ask You to set them apart for Your favor. No matter where they are now or how far they have wandered away, bless them back to You in such a way they know it is You alone.

Bless them when they go out into the workplace, the community, the places they enjoy, nature, and the entertainment they seek. Let them see, hear, taste, touch, and be drawn to You. And may they miss You and begin to look for a safe place in the presence of Your grace.

Bless them and their children. Let Your favor be with them when they eat and when they sleep, when they lie down and when they get up, when they have needs and You supply what is best for them. Bless them with their income potential, safety from their enemies, and peace—wonderful peace—that they find when they come in from all the cares of the world.

May their children bring them great joy, and may they live lives of gratitude every day of their lives for each other and You, Lord God.

Thank You for everything, negative and positive, in my life that has shaped my thinking and made me useful for Your purpose. I will not let others define me, I will not let Satan define me, I will not let me define me—only You, Lord, know what You made, and only You can define me. I am learning to like what I see; I am learning to like me. That's Your love and grace. I don't understand it, but I want to learn. So keep me vigilant against attacks formed against me with Your Word. Keep me looking forward to winning the race and to hear You say, "Well done."

In the name of the Father, the Son, and the Holy Spirit, amen.

God Shed His Grace on Me is God's divine revelation in my life. For His presence is the Scarlet Thread that runs through the pages. From the beginning to the day my life ends, I have a purpose to glorify Him and tell of His wonderful divine intervention in my blessed and grateful life. The label I wear is who I am—His for all eternity, and there will be no end.

This is who I am. I am the righteousness of God through Jesus Christ. I am redeemed by the blood of the Lamb, who died in my place so I could live. I am guided by His presence. He lives in me, and I can do anything He proposes for me to do. He said so, and I believe what He believes.

I am valuable. I have never been satisfactory to You, always priceless. I am made for excellence, and He won't lower the bar. For my God has filled me with His power and love. He has watched over me all the days of my life, steering me back when I wandered off, never out of His precious sight. No one could take my place; He made me one of a kind according to my DNA, His signature.

I have been picked up when I fell, encouraged when I got discouraged and sent back out to make my Father proud. Knowing His voice, loudest in the stands. Who am I? I am a child of God. I bring

Him joy, and He puts that joy in me. He defines me and labels me good, very, very good.

This is who I am. Though I have fallen short more than I have lived up to His high calling, He has never taken His eye off me, even when I took my eyes off Him. He never abandoned me when I thought I didn't need Him around that much.

The faith that I learned as a child, the faith that I saw demonstrated in my dad, who loved God with all his heart and loved others as God loved him—this is the reason that I write this book. This is the reason that I pass on the legacy that he passed on to me.

God shed His grace on me. Why? It is still a mystery to me. Who am I that the Creator of the Universe would take notice of me, would want to reveal Himself to me, would love me and love me so very much that He would never give up until He found me and brought me back to life?

This is my story. This is who I am, and this is what matters most to me. You matter to me. I love you and want you to know where you came from. The people who came before you and have prayed for you are intricately woven into the fabric of your life as well.

I am your mother, your grandmother, and your great-grandmother, and it is the desire of my heart that you will pass my story on to your children and all those who touch your lives.

My legacy of love is who I am, what I believe, and why. My highest calling is to hear, "Well done, my good and faithful servant. I trusted you with the lives I gave you to love and nurture, and you passed it down through a thousand generations."

I want you to know that God shed His grace on you and how He seeks to bring you into a personal relationship with Jesus, the One who loves you most. For His presence to be the Scarlet Thread that runs through the story of your life. My story continues through the lives of all of you… make it a good one!

To Our Family

The godly walk with integrity; blessed are their
children who follow them. (Proverbs 20:7 NLT)

Yesterday, as I unpacked boxes and boxes and even more boxes, memories of a lifetime swept over me. Should I keep this, throw that away, and make something new out of that tiny baby shoe? Things that meant so much to me may perhaps hold little meaning to you.

And that's the rub.

I have heard it said, and well, it seems to be true: a whole generation can pass before those you have loved, nurtured, and guided through those early years ever really listen to you. So for those who are listening, this is what I want you to know, and why it is important. Not just what I think, but life, as seen through my eyes.

I write to my children, my grandchildren, and now, my great-grandchildren. The first thing I know is I am old, old but not dead. It is the desire of my heart to leave my story to you that will outlast these few short years before eternity takes me to a world without end.

I am expecting you to join me. Be ready. I will be waiting. Until then…when you think of me, which I hope you do, maybe at Christmas or birthdays or perhaps when someone reminds you of me, I want you to know sharing life with you has been the best gift I've ever received.

You, my family, are my story. That story tells about my hopes, my dreams, and my prayers for you. Some prayers have been fulfilled, some are going through change, and some I may not realize until long after I leave this place.

Every memory I have of you brings such joy, and every struggle you go through I feel deeply. I have questioned many times, did I do enough to prepare you for the real world? Did I set a good example? I know I was a good mother and grandmother but not great. I made many mistakes, and God is straightening those crooked places out for me with the time I have left. It is very humbling. Being a perfect anybody is a goal that nobody can reach.

Picture this.

If God were to be sitting in our best comfortable chair this Christmas when gifts are exchanged, there would be the typical oohs and ahs for those shiny things everyone thinks they want, they need, and can't live without—at least until a new shiny thing that everyone wants, everyone needs, and can't live without comes out.

But this is what being old has taught me. In the vast expanse of this earth, we are like a moment in time. Everything that seems so important is important no more.

My life is like a tiny package. One side of the package is crushed; all the hopes and dreams have been altered by life's happenings. There is a rip in the pretty paper, and oh how I don't want anyone to see. The bow is smashed, and all the tape I've put on it is not working. I tug and pull and try to smooth out this gift. It's not good enough to give to those I love.

But you are in this life; you are the good part, the best part, the gift that has been given to me. Thinking of you and the memories of you are what makes me smile, and I know I did something right. I must have done a lot right.

I will always love you, and I give you to my loving Father, believing we will all be together in a better place, an eternal place where all my hopes, dreams, and prayers prayed for you over all these years are realized.

Beyond what we can even imagine, there is so much more than this.

I believe, dear children, I believe God has always had a reason to bring us into this world, to put us together as a family, grateful for each day and making it the best it was meant to be.

We learn from difficulties, and they have a purpose.

He is remaking us in His image. He sees what only He can see, and the picture is worth a thousand words. If we cooperate with the reshaping, we grow into Christlikeness and there is peace in trials, contentment for every day, and joy. Oh yes, joy!

He is picking us up, straightening us out with wise discipline, giving us just enough trouble to humble us, and blessing us with His mercy every morning.

You are my legacy and everything I've always wanted.

I thank my God every time I remember you.
In all my prayers for all of you, I always
pray with joy. (Philippians 1:3–4 NIV)

Remember Where
You Came From

First Love

I pray also that the eyes of your heart may be
enlightened in order that you may know the
hope to which he has called you, the riches
of his glorious inheritance in the saints,
and his incomparably great power for us
who believe. (Ephesians 1:18–19 NIV)

Dad—a son's first hero and a daughter's first love.

As I said at the beginning of this epistle, the story of my beginning, my daddy was the one who made the biggest impression on my life. My view of God today has shaped the person I am. He laid the foundation, and God arranged and rearranged all the pieces in this messy quilt that, if I had it to do over again, I would. But I can't. But God can, and He is.

Do-overs are His specialty, and that is why He came to give us new life. We are recreated, reborn. That is the good news, the best news, and that is the Gospel of Jesus Christ.

Nicodemus could not understand this and asked Jesus, "Can I go back into the womb and be born?" Jesus knew the things of this world cannot be understood with human wisdom. He said to him, "You must be born again to be able to enter the kingdom of God." He meant that Nicodemus must think differently; his thinking was natural, but when he is born again, he will experience a supernatural birth that will only happen when the Spirit of God comes into his life, his thinking, and his heart.

These things are foolishness to those who live in the natural, but to those who believe, it is the power of God. For a natural man or woman cannot understand the things of God. Nicodemus's life changed after that conversation recorded in the third chapter of John.

At first, he was afraid of what the other religious leaders would think and came to Jesus in the night. But later, he challenged those who sat on the Jewish council, and along with Joseph of Arimathea, asked for Jesus's body to prepare for burial. He was a changed person and showed great courage because of his new life in Christ.

And my life has changed too. I am thankful that I don't think the way I used to think or want to do the things that I used to want to do. The new me remembers what I have been through, and it keeps me humble, and it keeps me from ever wanting to return to that bondage of regrets that Jesus brought me through. It is part of my story, and so clear to me now as I remember the former days and all those "it's all about me" years.

For God came into this world in human flesh to be born as we are born, so we could be reborn to be like Him. He loves us that much. He loves us, accepts us, nurtures us, and wants us to have His nature living in us so we will love, accept, and nurture those who need to know Him.

Jesus came into this world to show His Father's love. He told the disciples, "Anyone who has seen me has seen the Father" (John 14:9). Jesus was showing them His Father's heart.

God has the heart of a father. I know that well. For my father was my role model who loved his God with all his heart and passed it down to me, his little girl. My father was my first love because my father first loved God, and it showed in everything he did, even when he thought I was not looking, Especially then…

Solid Rock

*I will show you what he is like who comes to
me and hears my words and puts them into
practice. He is like a man building a house
who dug down deep and laid the foundation
on rock. When a flood came, the torrent struck
that house but could not shake it, because
it was well built. (Luke 6:47–48 NIV)*

As I looked into the deep, dark hole, I silently cried out to the Lord, "This is the size of the hole in my heart. Will I ever feel peace and contentment as long as our son is in bondage to unbelief? How can I enjoy this wonderful blessing while he lives in complete darkness?"

Then God's gentle answer seemed to reply to my troubled soul as if He were enfolding me in His arms and whispering my name. "Look, My child, you are standing on holy ground."

The excavator walked over and said, "That rock is not going anywhere!" He then informed us that our new home would be built right on top of that solid rock foundation. The only visible part was the cornerstone firmly grounded and pointing toward the sky. He raised his arms as if to say, "Ta-da!"

To everyone within hearing range, what he said had no more significance than a weather forecast, a tidbit of information. But to those who recognized the voice of God through the obvious coincidences, there could be no mistake. God spoke, and in fact, He was singing to me, "The wise man built his house upon the rock, and the house on the rock stood sound."

Thoughts flooded my mind as I remembered being a six-year-old little girl skipping along, holding onto my daddy's hand. Each and every Sunday, and many days in between, we would walk the familiar path to the neighborhood church where dedicated Sunday school teachers taught me Bible stories about the faithfulness of a loving God.

How those little childhood songs would make us dance up and down, clapping our hands as we sang as loud as we could:

> "The wise man built his house upon the Rock,
> House upon the rock, house upon the rock
> The wise man built his house upon the rock,
> And the rains came tumbling down."
> (Little fingers waving, demonstrating the familiar song.)
> The rains came down and the floods came up
> The rains came down and the floods came up
> The rains came down, and the floods came up,
> And the house on the rock stood sound.
> But the foolish man who did not build his house upon the rock,
> His house fell down."

And that is when all the little children fell down in a muddy mess on the floor while giggling and rolling around.

Just as my Father had prepared a little six-year-old for the world I would be living in, my heavenly Father prepared me for the one that only He knew was to come. He knew that we would be building a house in a bad economy. He knew that we would question our sanity by building in a declining housing market and wondering if everything that we had saved for all our lives would come crashing down.

He knew about the beautiful dreams in my heart that would make me dance up and down and clap my hands because He had put those dreams in my heart. And He knew our son would be living away from all we taught him about God, and wondering if it was my fault, leaving me with this big emptiness in my heart—an ache that only He could fill.

Years ago, while I was pouring out my heart to God about finding contentment in the circumstances that were all around me, He seemed to say to my restless spirit and anxious heart, "I am in the process of teaching you, my child. This is going to take time—a long time; you are not ready."

Yet God intricately knows me; my mind is an open book (a good read). In fact, He put His best dreams there waiting for me to find them. So I asked right out loud, "When, Lord?" and I sensed His voice saying that I would learn contentment by persevering through the discontentment, and I had a lot to learn yet.

The doctor also said that to me when I was giving birth to my child. "You are not in hard labor yet."

I screamed, "You mean it is going to get worse?"

But that was not the end of the whining. I wanted to know why the lesson could not come easier and quicker. For some reason, I already knew what He would say. Something about being thankful; something about knowing who to be grateful to. Reminding me how I tend to take His credit for things or think that I am "so smart." I know, I know.

But I had one more thing to say, "What if the good things are not what look so good to me?" He waited for me to be quiet and just think about what I had said. It seemed like a long time—but at least I was paying attention. Then even though there was no audible sound, He whispered to this mother's heart, "If you do not enjoy giving yucky stuff to your children, why would I?" He made His point!

A couple of days ago, I was looking back through my prayer journals, reading all the epistles that I had written to God over the years. I seemed to be doing all the talking—little listening, I am sorry to say. But then, my eyes fell on a scripture that I felt God had given me. There was a date on it and a thank you written beside it.

At that time, I did not know when or what, but I thanked Him for what I could not see, knowing that it would come. And I would recognize it when the time came. The verse was about boundary lines falling in delightful places. There have been so many detours and places that have turned out not to be delightful that I said, "Lord, please make it obvious to me. Remember how hard it is for me to 'get it.'"

Then when we were able to buy the four acres with the mountain view overlooking Moose Hollow (that we would not have been able to afford if it had not been a bad economy), I could not have been happier. The dream that He put in my heart so long ago was exactly what made me jump up and down like a silly girl.

Everything was there. The private hiking trails with blackberry bushes, lots of maple, oak, and white birches that nature placed at the exact spot to add to the beauty without blocking the sun, a mountain stream with a babbling brook while songbirds sing songs of praise each day, and a 360-degree scenic view of rolling hills and a winding road lined with my own historical stone wall, nestled in just the right place like a window on my heaven on earth. A sweet taste of what resembles the English countryside that I have always loved would one day be the place I would call…home.

But it could be a coincidence. I needed a sign, a sign with His fingerprints on it. I have a lot to learn about being in the perfect will of God and not my own, which never ends up with contentment but more lessons to learn—been there!

So I waited for God to make the next move. I would not buy this picture-perfect land that takes care of its own landscaping unless He could make it obvious. And He seemed to say that He had given me His best and signed it with His very own hand. Did I think it was a coincidence that our last name and the name of the picture-perfect road were the same? For our name was the name of the road?

No one else has ever lived on this land. He had saved it for just such a time as this to be the answer to our prayer, and His answer has His fingerprints everywhere.

As I gazed over the beautiful landscape before me, my thoughts returned to a time when we met a woman in the countryside of England. As we were talking on a cobblestone road in Bath, she smiled with a big grin on her face and said, "I love your laugh!" Her beautiful English accent was charming, and it made me laugh again. But what God wanted me to hear through this sweet, delightful woman is that He loves to hear me laugh too!

And He loves to give us the desires of our hearts because He loves us. He wants to hear us sing for Him, jump up and down like silly children clapping our hands with joy and having fun, delighted with the good things He has done for you and me. And He loves to hear our stories coming from our grateful hearts. The things we enjoy in our children, God does too!

Delight yourselves in the Lord and He will give
you the desires of your heart. (Psalm 37:4)

A New Perspective

Bless the Lord, O my soul, and all that is
within me, bless his holy name Bless the Lord,
O my soul, and forget not all his benefits, who
forgives all your iniquity, who heals all your
diseases, who redeems your life from the pit, who
crowns you with steadfast love and mercy, who
satisfies you with good things so that your youth
is renewed like the eagle's. (Psalm 103:3–4)

Many decades ago, when we lived in Kansas City, we taught the Bible to young children of various ages and at various times. One particular Sunday, my marine was teaching a group of middle school boys, just as I had seen my own dad do through previous decades of my life. When my husband, the marine, asked the boys, "Who wrote the Psalms?" the answer they immediately gave was Barry Manilow.

Now that was and still is too funny.

So I got to thinking, after all the things we have persevered through, as far back as I can remember, and even back to the days of David who originally wrote the Psalms. What would it mean to people who would read it far into the future? He was just praying this private prayer and praising God for all that he had learned about the love and goodness of God. And that is why I am passionate about what I write and leave for my children and grandchildren for years, and hopefully decades to come: my story of a Father's love for me.

I know if I were writing the Psalms, I might look over the journey of my life and say something like…

The Lord is my real estate agent. The market is always in my favor.

He makes me rest each night in the house of my dreams, surrounded by beautifully landscaped gardens, and when I wake, the smell of coffee revives my soul. Yeah, when the time is right, my phone rings with multiple offers for His namesake, revealing His personal involvement in what I accomplish.

Though the housing market looks bleak to others, and the economy is on a downward slide, I refuse to fear or participate. He walks me through job changes, health issues, and even retirement; I never become their victim, for He is providing direction and new opportunities I see. He provides the right amount of sunshine and rain to fall on my anointed head.

At the end of the day, my agent leaves me the key to His own house with heavenly upgrades. He invites me to live with Him forever.

Dear Lord, thank You for a better attitude. We both know that I have not always had one. Encourage me to stay focused on You when life doesn't resemble the picture I've painted.

Eternally grateful,
Linda

Below the Surface

*Again, Jesus spoke to them saying, "I am
the light of the world. Whoever follows me
will never walk in darkness but will have
the light of life." (John 8:12 NRSV)*

How quickly we can see something that we do not agree with and just automatically assume that something is not right. After all, we know it all, and if it doesn't fit what we know, then it is wrong. Right? Can we just admit that we do not know it all? Can we try to see the point that is the bigger point and not take the point out of context?

There are opportunities every day to look below the surface and understand, not just with the head but with the heart. Having a relationship is more important than winning an argument, outsmarting someone, or being a better debater. We could win that battle and still lose. I've been there; maybe you have too.

Common knowledge says that something happens, and then something else follows. We want God to write the way we think, sort of bringing Him down to our level instead of helping us to see things from His. But God does not limit Himself by being logical and rational just because we want life to be logical and rational according to how we think. He wants all of us to live in the supernatural, and to think outside the box.

The Bible is full of promises and principles that will give us the supernatural wisdom and understanding that we need when we seek first after His own heart. For example, we want good things to happen to good people. But God says that none of us are good, no not one (Romans 1:3). Now I know a lot of people who claim to be good, and they do appear to live good lives. They think they are good and have convinced us that they are good because they do good things.

And some really good-for-nothing people think they are good because they haven't done anything bad or as bad as the other guy.

But God said no one is good, that we all fall short of being good because He sees the heart, the motive. He sees below the surface. And if those good things that we think are good become too hard to do, we will just lower the bar. Now the bad things that we didn't use to do because they were not good, are now good and we are now good. See how this works?

And if we do not understand the things of God, because they are not logical and rational according to us, and they do not look good anymore for us to do or not to do, we want to lower the bar. So what do we do?

We say the Bible has *mistakes* and use the same question from Genesis that Satan put into the heart of man, "Did God really say that?" And all through history that question, of whether we can really trust God and believe in His authority, has been the central question. And do we see how this works again?

We will just quit God altogether and find a better god—one that is more to our own liking and says what we want to hear. And that drumbeat goes on and on. Are we better off getting rid of God and becoming our own god? Absolutely not! Oh, now there's the rub. Absolutes absolutely did not look good anymore, so now we are free to make good anything we want it to be. Here we go again.

Well, it is time to go and pull the weeds out of my garden. I don't believe in weeds, and I have no use for weeds, but they still appear in my garden. I will just lower the bar and decide that I love weeds and believe that they should be in my garden and that choking out the plants is not as harmful as it has always been, and then I will be happy! This may not be true, but I will say it is true and then I will be happy. But sometimes, I do wonder if God ever says to Himself that weeds were a mistake. Oh, probably not because there were no weeds in that very first garden.

We first stopped believing, and then there were weeds. Genesis does not say that exactly, but it is there if you look below the surface.

You shall seek Me and find Me, when you seek
for Me with all your heart; And I will be found
by you, says the Lord. (Jeremiah 29:13)

This is a promise of restoration after the completion of the time allotted for discipline due to their rebellion. We should read this verse as pertaining not only to them but to all people in Old Testament days and today. God has made Himself completely and totally available to those who want to know Him.

The fool says in his heart, "There is no God." But wisdom comes from God, and those who are wise seek Him and will want to go deeper—to see things through the eyes of God.

All my life, I have heard that God is love and that God loves me. I accepted it without question, but not anymore. Now I want to know why. Who am I that He should love me? This mystery makes me go deeper, and the answer is why I so love Him, and I will follow Him wherever He goes.

The song we sang in that little church when I was growing up means more today than ever before because I have experienced His leading me through the last seventy years.

Wherever He leads, I'll go, Wherever He leads
I'll go, I'll follow my Christ, who loves me so,
wherever He leads I'll go.

Weeds in My Garden

Jesus told them another parable: The kingdom of heaven is like a man who sowed good seed in his field. But while everyone was sleeping, his enemy came and sowed weeds among the wheat, and went away...the servants asked him, "Do you want us to go and pull them up?" "No," he answered, "because while you are pulling the weeds, you may root up the wheat." (Matthew 13:24–30)

Now if you are not a student of the Bible or grew up hearing this story in the little church where these stories are a staple in your spiritual growth, you may not know what is being taught by Jesus in this verse to those who came to hear and ask questions.

On the surface, it would seem obvious that Jesus is giving them tips on gardening—how to have the best crops and get your picture on the front of *Better Homes and Gardens* with the biggest tomatoes and the most beautiful roses that would surely win a ribbon at the town fair.

But that would be missing the point. Jesus is talking about good and evil. Yes, the same good and evil that are still around today. We have made evil smell better and given it a new name that is softer on the eyes and easier to swallow. But hard as each generation tries to make good in their own eyes look and sound good, it is still smelly and just as ugly as it was before.

We all know instinctively what is right but pretend that we don't. Tolerance is just another name for nothing else to lose, and then the weeds in this generation are bored and have to burn something down. Then what? Is anything different? Has anything gotten better? For a time, some may feel better, but not deep within, where it really matters. And that is a battle with the weeds that we ourselves cannot win.

So what the weeds represent can be anything that sets itself up against the knowledge of God. The discerning spirit knows that no matter what we call something, we know it is skewed and trying to make good fit wrong and wrong fit good—like putting a square peg in a round hole.

We have to jump through a lot of hoops to make it look, taste, smell, and feel right. Jesus taught the meaning of this parable to His disciples and to all of us who are trying to live for the kingdom of God in an ungodly world.

> *So He explained. "The farmer who sows the pure*
> *seed is the Son of Man. The field is the world,*
> *the pure seeds are subjects of the kingdom, the*
> *thistles are subjects of the Devil, and the enemy*
> *who sows them is the Devil. The harvest is the*
> *end of the age, the curtain of history. The harvest*
> *hands are angels." (Matthew 13:37–39 MSG)*

They lived with injustice, and they worked alongside the propaganda of their time. The scribes and Pharisees, who were the *know-it-alls* of their day, were the worst at getting good and evil backward. Their good was for show and came from nothing but a desire for praise and admiration. They wanted more to be praised and worshiped, admired by the elites of their day, in the synagogue and the government. Fast-forward, and it's the same evil in our government elites. And everyone who has a platform to preach or sits in a Sunday pew is not a believing saint.

Now you may be thinking, *Well, who does she think she is?* I know, I am guilty too. I like to fit in, not make waves. I want people to like me and think I am as good or at least not as bad as that fellow over there. But that discerning spirit that is a good thing when we see things from God's point of view is also a curse when we don't want to. It leaves a bad taste in my mouth and weeds in the garden of my life that are choking out any good I might do.

Jesus is answering the question His disciples asked about what to do about the evil around them. The permissive attitudes, the idol worship, the anti-God culture that was becoming the new norm. Shouldn't we just call fire down from heaven and burn them all up was a question of one or two disciples who had had enough. Yeah, I've felt that way too.

Now I don't know if Jesus thought this was funny as I first did, but He patiently heard their frustration and wanted them to know that life is hard, and we must be patient in waiting for God's time. He said to leave the weeds and let the evil grow right alongside those who are trying to do what is right. If we try to pull out the weeds, the tangled roots under the ground may accidentally pull out the wheat that represents the good. But in the end, all will be pulled out and separated. The good will be rewarded for the good and faithful lives they have led, and the evil will be punished severely for all eternity for all the harm they have done to others and for rebelling against the good and rejecting God.

What are the weeds in our lives? Maybe we work in an environment that is hostile to our faith, and it gets harder and harder to get up and do what God has called us to do. Maybe everywhere we look, there are unfulfilled expectations or relationships that would be easier if we could just turn our backs on them.

And maybe we are part of the problem. We have blended in so much that we look like everyone else. We have toxic relationships, we don't do what we should but what everyone else says is perfectly okay, and everything is totally repackaged to make evil look good. We become lazy and disorganized, eat unhealthy foods, or eat only what we are told to eat, and somehow that makes us feel better than everyone who doesn't do what they are told to do.

Whether it is the worship of idols, our own body image, or whatever weeds we think we can't live with or without, we still have to deal with ourselves. So are we part of the weeds or are we the good wheat? For if we look under the surface, Jesus will show us the answer we seek.

What Do You Want?

*Seek first the Kingdom of God and His
Righteousness, and all these things will be
given to you as well. (Matthew 6:33 NIV)*

The question I asked God so many years ago now, "What if the good things You give me don't look so good to me?" brings tears to my eyes because the wisdom I did not know then, He now pours into that empty place in my soul. God whispers that His thoughts are higher than my thoughts, His ways are higher than my ways. He knows what I cannot, and who among us can say, "O God, what have You done?"

God does not owe us a reason. Why the parents He chose for some may or may not be a good fit or why we do not have the option to pick a new set in the fine print. He does not check in to see if it is a convenient time to fit a child into our lives or explain why, when we plead for a baby to hold, His answer is still no. He doesn't ask our permission when there are lessons to learn; He doesn't debate with us over our income or lack thereof. Why He heals some but not others.

Why do the wicked prosper and the saints suffer? There must be something we cannot see. What do we believe about God? Is He good? Is He? Yes, God is good; God is perfect in all of His ways. He knows what He is doing, and to question that seems a bit arrogant to me. He knows where He is leading and what lies ahead that we cannot. He knows when we are able to take the next step and when the next step would be beyond what we could bear.

He may lead us to an understanding but not always. There are things that our minds can't take in, things only He can know. He may send others to teach us, warn us, or be a good example for us, but our greatest knowledge comes by walking through the experience and then passing that wisdom learned along.

We are a stubborn, rebellious people, and we suffer through the consequences that we face in everyday life when we fail to listen to what we know is right. That's me, and maybe you?

Yet some things may not be our fault; someone else caused the grief we bear. What's with that? You try to do what's right, and bad things still happen to good people, and good things happen to bad people. It doesn't seem fair.

Now I know what I didn't know then: that the lessons were not for me alone, but for those who follow. When given the things that did not make sense, the things unfair, the pain without seeing the gain, or the door shut when opened wide to others, what did they see, the ones that followed? Did my faith become stronger? Was I a wimp or a whiner, or when all that life threw to distract me, and the challenges attacked me, did I come through a winner?

The role models in my life suffered through hardship and pain. Life was not easy; they lived through a depression and never took their next meal for granted. They were thankful and didn't blame God or ask Him if He could be trusted. They knew, and they were teaching me to love and trust Him too.

When God did not give them the answer to their prayer, they never thought He didn't love them and that He didn't care. They believed that things would be different in a day up ahead, and even if not, it didn't matter. Their faith grew through adversity and became stronger.

We watched the celebration of the life of Brian Avery, a godly man who we were privileged to learn from every Tuesday night through his vast Bible knowledge. Whether on the mission field abroad or teaching at our church, his life was a testimony of his love for God that was contagious. It made us hunger to know more and more about our Lord and Friend. If you can do that when you meet others, there is no higher calling in your life, no greater joy you can give.

I reminded myself that God doesn't call the equipped, but He equips the called. And I know if anyone reads what I am writing and it makes a difference in their life, if they want to know who my God is, then I have truly been blessed because I was used to be a blessing to others when I introduced them to Jesus Christ.

I have lived over seventy years, and for pretty much all that time, I have been training to be of some good for a purpose I could not see. I must admit, if I had not taken my own wrong turns many times, I could have knocked off about forty years of boot camp and gotten to the finish line with less baggage.

I have been writing this note and that journal entry for decades. Some have been so long ago that I had to change the date from twenty years ago to thirty or fifty years ago. I should have left the date blank. Some of the names I purposely left blank to protect the innocent and the guilty and details were put in when necessary but left out when it would hurt more than help. Too much information is still too much information.

It is the heart of God that inspires what I write. He made Brian a teacher to thousands, and He gave me a love for writing. When Jesus asked the crippled man if he wanted to walk, was he willing to not just beg for money from those who passed by, or, as I would paraphrase it, did he want to walk badly enough that come hell or high water, he believed that he could do just that. Jesus's next words were, "Pick up your mat and walk," and that is what happened. He walked.

So many years ago, I sat and thought about all that life gave or did not give to me—the highs and lows, the good times or the not-so-good times—and what I had learned, what it all meant. It was as if Jesus were saying to me, "Write it down. Do you want to tell your children and grandchildren things they may never know about you? Who you are, what you believe in, and why it matters?"

Jesus saw me before I was even born and knew every day before even one was ever written. On the thirteenth day of January, on a Friday, just before the clock would turn over to a day with a less negative tone attached to it, I came into this world. I came into this world to be a writer, a writer for Him.

It is my purpose, my calling, and my privilege to hear Jesus say to me, "Do you want to be a writer? Pick up your pen and write your story, the one I have been writing on your heart."

My life's story is one that I am still writing. It is my desire to seek first the kingdom of God and His righteousness, and what I want more than anything is a legacy of faith that will be remembered long after I am gone.

> We're pilgrims on the journey of the narrow road,
> And those who've gone before us line the way,
> Cheering on the faithful, encouraging the weary,
> Their lives a stirring testament to God's sustain-
>   ing grace.
>
> O may all who come behind us find us faithful,
> May the fire of our devotion light their way.
> May the footprints that we leave lead them to
>   believe,
> And the lives we live inspire them to obey.
> O may all who come behind us find us faithful.
>
> Surrounded by so great a cloud of witnesses,
> Let us run the race not only for the prize,
> But as those who've gone before us.
> Let us leave to those behind us,
> The heritage of faithfulness
> Passed on through godly lives.
>
> After all our hopes and dreams have come and gone,
> And our children sift through all we've left behind,
> May the clues that they discover,
> And the mem'ries they uncover,
> Become the light that leads them,
> To the road, we each must find.
>
> May all who come behind us find us faithful...
> (Steven Green)

Same Old, Same Old

*That which has been what will be, That which
is done is what will be done, And there is
nothing new under the sun. (Ecclesiastes 1:9)*

The marine who had shared the last fifty years of my life story was pumping gas into his truck when, across the parking lot, the chief of police noticed him and hurried over. "Now what had he done?" was a question on his mind.

"I see from your license plate that you served in Vietnam, and I just wanted to shake your hand and thank you for your service to our country." He returned his handshake and thanked him for the kind words of appreciation.

"Not too many of you guys left," he said, and the marine agreed that time was passing fast.

His thoughtful words to the man I love meant even more to me. He didn't have to; he could have just gone on his way, not something he needed to do to comply with a company policy to "thank a vet" today. It felt heartfelt and meant so much. So much to the marine who spent years in the wet rice paddies during monsoon season, crawling through the jungle, trying to hear the sounds of those trying to capture or kill him. He was there for the right reason, to help those oppressed to live free.

I remember when I first met the marine. The hostile, angry mobs called those who served murderers. How ugly their accusations were. There may have been some bad apples, but they painted all with the same broad brush. I guess this is human nature; there will always be people who need to have a cause that makes them feel better about themselves. If they can riot and scream at others, they feel they have become better in their own eyes.

But their hostility never seemed to be satisfied. No matter what they thought they achieved, they were still angry. They were miserable and unhappy and wanted everyone else to be miserable and unhappy. It was a vicious cycle, and no matter what the year or decade, the beat went on, and there was nothing new under the sun, as Solomon said a long, long time ago.

The culture is out of control, bitterness rages, and there are those behind the safety of their newsrooms egging them on. The riots of today and the riots of 1968 are the same. What has changed? Are we better with all our counseling, all our political correctness, all our finger-pointing, and tongues wagging, and throwing more and more money to make taxpayers pay for things that have never worked and, the dirty secret, were never meant to?

The issue of hate is big business; it sells, and it keeps people in power and in office election after election. Just fueling the hate and the promise for change doesn't need to produce—just say whatever. And the beat goes on, and no one seems to catch on that they are being duped.

I listen to little of what they have to say. I like the peace and quiet, and I think I shall keep it that way. The name-calling and shouting each other down is something I've had quite enough of. What a waste of time, and time is not something we can replace. It comes around once and then it's gone. The people that we have loved, so many are not around the table anymore. Seems like every year, one more friend has left to be with the Lord, their free upgrade from all this dysfunction down here.

But before I fall into the trap of thinking I am above it all, I admit my own tunnel view. Thinking that my knight in shining armor might be too good to be true and I might be heading into yet another mistake, I put my worst step forward to discover the cracks in the responsible, mature human being who always put me first and treated me with the respect that naturally came through.

But the marine and I are celebrating fifty years this June, so needless to say, we made it work. Can't think of much we haven't done that is left on that bucket list. But we are living the best years of our lives right now, listening to God and using these days to serve Him with hearts of gratitude, doing each new day better than the day before.

We are using what we have learned, staying focused on what really matters, and persevering through what does not. And until we leave our place at the table, we are more than content.

Something that is a fact is that God does more with what we have left than all the years before. The Bible shows example after example of people who were used in a mighty way for God's purpose in their advanced years. So who knows what He has planned for us, but it will be fun to find out.

Grow old with me; the best is yet to be.

God's Craftsmanship

The heavens are telling the glory of God; they are a marvelous display of His craftsmanship. Day and night they keep on telling about God. Without a sound or word, silent in the skies, their message reaches out to all the world. The sun lives in the heavens where God placed it. (Psalm 19:1–4 TLB)

In Old Testament scriptures, David, who spent his days under the sun and nights under the stars keeping watch over the sheep, felt the presence of God in everything and everywhere he looked. God was speaking to His humble servant, and He was making it clear. He created all that could be seen and all that was too vast to see by his frail humanity. God's plan was miraculous and all fit together by the Designer's perfect plan. David could not help but worship and praise Him, and out of that, he could not help but sing about and write songs about all that amazed him.

The book that I love to read and reread again and again is *Growing Strong in the Seasons of Life* by Charles R. Swindoll. I am always blessed and strengthened by the practical wisdom that I am apt to forget with my limited scope of understanding and the focus I need always to maintain. Then I too worship and praise my God for keeping this world under His control and keeping me in awe of all that I can't understand when my personal world seems to be out of control. I know whose hand holds my tiny hand.

In this book, there is an illustration that speaks to this vast universe where we have such a small speck in which we dwell. The reason it moves me to such an extent is perhaps because all that we know defies rational explanation, just like my prayers have done for me so many times in the past. This was also the conclusion made by Dr. A.

Cressy Morrison, a noted scientist and former president of the New York Academy of Sciences. I will quote his words on page 393:

> To deny that these worlds beyond the lens are the results of God's design is to defy all mathematical calculations of chance.

He illustrates this by saying,

> Suppose I would take ten pennies and mark them from 1 to 10 and give them to you to put into your pocket. I'd ask you to give them a good shake then I'd say, "I'm going to reach into your pocket and draw out penny number 1." My chance of doing this would be 1 in 10 if I accomplished it. And then I have you put number 1 back in your pocket, have you shake them again, and I'd say, "I will now draw out number 2." My chances are much slimmer 1 in 100.
>
> And then do the same with number 3, it would be 1 in 1000. If I draw out each number in order, following the identical process, the ultimate chance factor would reach the unbelievable figures of 1 chance in 10 billion!

You would think the game is fixed. That's exactly what I am saying about the galaxies and the germs, and more importantly, your life and mine on this earth. The arrangement is fixed—there is a Designer, God, and He is not silent. As a matter of fact, He declares His presence twenty-four hours a day.

> *The heavens declare the glory of God; the skies*
> *proclaim the work of His hands. Day after*
> *day they pour forth speech; night after night*
> *they display knowledge. There is no speech or*

language where their voice is not heard. Their voice goes out into all the earth, their words to the ends of the world. In the heavens He has pitched a tent for the sun. (Psalm 19:1–4 NIV)

And that is too marvelous, too wonderful, too amazing for me to understand. But I am not God, and neither are you. God has made Himself known, and the only thing that defeats that is our own stubborn pride. For if we open our eyes, there is all the proof we will ever need.

The Rest of the Story

Unfailing love and truth have met together.
Righteousness and peace have kissed!
Truth springs up from the earth, and righteousness
smiles down from heaven. (Psalm 85:10–11 NLT)

I reviewed and revised my bucket list today—things to do before time and years get away. Oh, I've mentally done that before, but there's something about putting it in writing that adds value to it, not just wishes, but goals. Funny how those wishes have changed. What seemed important at one point, what others were doing or striving for, now seems to be nothing more than busyness. The race we are in with the other rats did not meet our high expectations.

If my life had a credit score, what would it say about how I lived it? To the full or running on fumes? How did I invest in the importance of each new day? Did I act justly, love mercy, and walk humbly with my God?

I wonder if God has a bucket list for me. What would be there that would make Him smile? I know—when I did the same thing He would do to show the love of Christ.

Life...

Have you ever read a book or started watching a movie and said, "I've seen this before"? I bet we all have at one time or another. Yet we may keep on reading or watching because we're not sure. Same storyline, perhaps, different time, place, and people, but you're sure you've seen it before. And you know how this thing is going to end, and you want everyone who hasn't seen it or heard it to know how it's going to end. And if someone tells us how it ends, it spoils the end. Don't we hate that when people do that? Yes, we do.

And then there are the times that you are reading along, and the lights go out, or the TV screen goes blank just when it was getting oh so good. What happened? We scream at the flat-screen TV that knows even less than we do. The interruption put finding out on hold. Maybe it was a power out, a technology glitch, or something in life that just butted in. But you want to know what happened next. Did they find their lost love? Forgive each other? Did they live? Did they survive? Who did it and why? Did the good win and did the bad pay a price?

We are left on the edge of our chair, saying that isn't fair. No answer to who, when, or why. We're left with the unanswered question of what happened.

But if you know the author of life, there will be no end. No end to the story because we turn a page on this life with all the misspelled words, the lines in our story we wish we never said, and the chapter in our "know it all" years that were costly. But there were also so many joys—they seemed to run parallel. Times of peace in the midst of the storm, times of rest when life ran amok, and then, God threw in grandchildren to make amok your favorite thing to do.

No, I wouldn't change one day. Not one single one. They all had their place and there was not one that was a waste. For all things worked according to His plan. He threw nothing away from the day I was born. For God knew I would need this to learn that.

He gathered every supply before my very first cry: the parents and friends, the teachers and preachers, the children, and grandchildren with their little fingers and especially their toes to step on everything I needed to know.

For we are a work in progress, and as long as we breathe, we are never quite finished with becoming our best you and me. To be better at anything takes a long, long time, and with each tiny step forward, we will trip a few times.

> For it is by grace you have been saved, through
> faith—and this not from yourselves, it is the gift

of God—not by works, so that no one can boast.
For we are God's workmanship, created in Christ
Jesus to do good works, which God prepared in
advance for us to do.

Another version of this verse says we are God's masterpiece.
That describes our worth, our value to the One who has intrinsically
been involved in every day of my life and yours. I recognize His
presence and clearly see how He has personally given me everything
I ever wanted because those things were in His plan.

The last chapter in this story is yet to be written, and the time
left to do it is certainly uncertain; but hopefully, with God's grace, it
will see pen to paper. Yet one thing I know: when I turn the last page
of my presence on earth, eternity starts where earth left off.

For now, I can only imagine what I will see. Waiting for me will
be family and friends.

My dad, the best role model of God this girl could ever have,
and my mother, excited to introduce my daughter, Hannah Grace.
And we know, without even saying, that her grandson will find the
Way.

And it seemed like yesterday when I said goodbye to my friends
and my teacher Mrs. Perry with a big grin on her face. And then
dancing to a heavenly band will be my dear friend Suzanne. All the
ones I've loved through all the years will hold a special gathering
with the saints I've read about. What an awesome time to actually be
greeted by Peter, Paul, John, Esther, Mary, and Ruth. The banquet
hall has been prepared and filled with the best of everything—new
sights and smells, and scrumptious food, beautifully displayed, with
ones we never knew existed.

I don't know what I shall wear, and I don't even care.

Then the party is roaring—it's full speed ahead with singing,
laughing, and hugging our loved ones and friends who shared with
us those few short years. And we will meet new brothers and sisters
too, from the beginning of time. Those cheering us on as we strug-

gled with struggles that seemed to go on and on, but when the race on earth was over, we won!

My life had a purpose beyond what I could see. I was never meant to be satisfied with a satisfactory me or live a life of mediocrity.

Then the most beautiful sight to behold is to look on the face of the One who saved me by His grace, and hear Him say, "My child, welcome home."

Tragedy Strikes

*God is our refuge and strength, a very present help
in trouble. Therefore, we will not fear, though
the earth should change, though the mountains
shake in the heart of the sea, though its waters
roar and foam, though the mountains tremble
with its tumult. (Psalm 46:1–3 NRSV)*

Faith's only function is to receive what grace
offers. (John Stott)

The headlines on the early morning news showed a tragedy that happened in the night. A massive bridge in Baltimore collapsed when a boat caught part of the bridge and brought it down. An image flashed in my mind of the panicked people on the bridge clinging to their lives or plunging into the icy waters; some were rescued, but others did not survive. This tragic accident came out of nowhere. Some died within minutes, and others prayed their last thoughts.

I remember growing up in Kansas City. Our family tragically lost a family member when the father and son were coming in from the farm. Lightning struck the son and he instantly died. His devastated father carried him back in his arms to his mother, who had been expecting them soon.

And two young men in our family were hit by a train. I didn't know them well because I was too small, but it is one of those things that you never forget. The details of what happened are now fuzzy at best, but it was what people talked about and wondered why.

After I graduated from Southeast High and was working for an investment company in the Crown Center area of Kansas City, Missouri, another tragedy occurred in the luxurious Hyatt Regency

Hotel. Everyone was in the pavilion of the hotel, with people so crowded that they were everywhere. It was a really good time for all as they swayed to the music from the overhead suspended decks that surrounded the inside of the hotel. Suddenly, everything and everyone on the decks came crashing down on top of all the people on the dance floor. So much death.

I was born after the war and didn't experience Pearl Harbor as my parents and grandparents did, but I was here when the Twin Towers came down. I was waiting to hear if my husband made it out of New York. He worked on Seventh Avenue, very near where the planes purposely flew into the buildings. It was several hours later in the day when someone was able to let me know that he was alive and would make it out of the city whenever he could.

The train station that he left to go to work that morning was still filled with cars three weeks later from those who never made it back. We grieved for our friends and neighbors who lost their lives. We grieved for our country, and we knew we would never forget.

Tragedy strikes. It doesn't give us a warning. It doesn't care. Rich or poor, successful or not, White or Black, kids or not, it does not favor one group over another. It only knows that eventually, your time is up. Death is a sure thing; no one gets a pass.

People ask why. Tragedy from storms that left destruction in its path, or pure evil that took their loved ones, and why, when God in His sovereignty could have prevented it from happening, why to them, to ones so young or good?

Death is inevitable. Some live to be old, and some die young, but despite taking good care of our health, having good genes, or staying away from the wrong place at the wrong time, we don't have much say in the matter. Only Jesus predicted His death, burial, and resurrection and pulled it off just as He said. And that is why the Son of God came, to die so even when we die, we shall live. Three Gospels tell this good news: Matthew 16:21–26, Mark 8:31–37, and Luke 9:22–25.

*Reminds me of the story in Scripture of Martha
and her sister, Mary. Their brother Lazarus had
become sick and was dying. They sent word to
Jesus that the one you love is sick and then they
waited expecting Him to come. But He didn't
come until it was too late. (John 11:1–44)*

All the sisters knew was that if Jesus had come, their brother
would be alive. Jesus gave them no explanation. He didn't say, "I was
healing a man who had been born blind and answering the charges
against Me from the spiritually blind religious leaders who were using
a good thing and calling it evil."

He didn't excuse Himself by mentioning that He had saved a
woman who was charged with adultery and about to be stoned to
death. He had asked that only the one who had never sinned cast the
first stone. Jesus knew their sins were great, and they knew too. He
saved her life from the angry mob, forgave her sins, and said, "Go
and sin no more." He didn't say adultery is fine or it's all about your
truth or mine. He forgave her and saved her life forever.

Now only God can forgive sins, and that is who Jesus is. There
was no doubt to those who could see, and the religious leaders hated
Him even more and continued to plot to take Him out.

All these things were happening before He finally arrived at the
home of His friends. He gave no answer to the sisters as to why He
was just now getting to them. Did He not understand how urgent it
was? I know I have asked that question too. I prayed and waited and
waited for my answer that didn't come. Have you?

But there is a reason even when we cannot know.

The sisters believed in life after death and knew that Lazarus
would live again, but they could not conceive of this happening
before their very eyes. But that is what they saw, and that is why
Jesus let this deep loss occur. Not only to demonstrate who He was
but also that He had the power over death. Lazarus had been in the
grave for three days, leaving no doubt that death had the final say.

Jesus called out, "Lazarus, come forth!" And Lazarus came walking out of the tomb.

Then Jesus asked those around to remove the cloth and linens that physically bound him. He included others in what He was doing. He has called us also, commissioned us to minister to the needs around us, both the physical needs and the spiritually bound, to the things that keep them from knowing the truth that sets the captives free.

All have sinned and fall short of the
glory of God. (Romans 1:23)

For the wages of sin is death, but the
gift of God is eternal life through Jesus
Christ, our Lord. (Romans 6:23)

If you confess with your mouth that Jesus is Lord
and believe in your heart that God raised him from
the dead, you will be saved. (Romans 10:9 NLT)

If we confessed our sins, he is faithful
to forgive us and cleanse us from all
unrighteousness. (1 John 1:9)

We have been set free! I know; this happened to me! I am part of the family of God, and Jesus prays for me, and I pray for you. And if you have asked Jesus to be your Savior, Jesus prays for you as well.

Holy Father, keep them and care for them—
all those you have given Me—so that they
will be united just as we are... I am praying
not only for these disciples but also for all
who will ever believe in Me because of
their testimony. (John 17:11, 20 NLT)

Tragedies of all kinds happen; it's life. Random acts of violence are on the rise and, in this current culture, often go unpunished, emboldening the thief, the rapist, and the murderer at an alarming rate. And if that were not enough to admit there is a serious problem, we are told it's our fault and not the fault of those who do evil things.

Jesus said,

> In this world we will have trouble but take heart
> He has overcome the world.

And there are three hundred and sixty-five verses in Scripture that reassure us and tell us not to worry about anything. We are secure because this world is temporary anyway, and those who believe have the hope of a better tomorrow.

Climate change is the religion of the day, but our God is Lord over the climate and has proclaimed that if the earth changes and the mountains quake, we are not to fear. He is our refuge and our strength.

God is our strength when tragedies strike. He is our ever-present help in whatever the future holds. We do not think like the world thinks and become frightened by the news of the day. Our hope comes from the promises of the One who holds our days in His hands, this day and through all the tomorrows of eternity!

Salvation of Our Soul

Most people embrace the assumption that God saves good people. So be good! Be moral. Be honest. Be decent. Pray the rosary. Keep the Sabbath. Keep your promises. Pray five times a day facing east. Stay sober. Pay taxes. Earn merit badges.

> But salvation of the soul is unearned. A gift. Our merits merit nothing. God's work merits everything. (Max Lucado)

Just thinking about my friend Jessie the other day. What a good friend and tons of fun, and also tons of advice. She is a nationally certified counselor, retired, a devoted woman of God by grace, and a mighty generous servant of Jesus whom she loves. I am blessed to know her and spend hours sharing, caring, and learning from her life experiences.

This last summer, we were putting together her life story in pictures in a collage while she spent the week with us. We all got into the arts and crafts project, and it was a beautiful time together, learning more about the wonderful Frank she was married to, who had recently passed away to be ushered into heaven's door.

It took hours to get those memories just right for the celebration of his life service we would be having the next day. All the preparations went together perfectly; it was a beautiful tribute to Frank's service to this country, complete with a military color guard playing taps. The meticulous folding of the flag, the salute, and its presentation to his beloved wife were so meaningful.

So it got me thinking. While I am on this earth, I want to be part of choosing the pictures that might be put on display by those who know me. The pictures that mattered the most to me, the pictures of the good times and laughs we have had over all the many years, our family, and dearest friends who have been with me to the end.

219

As I am getting on in years, I have passed the average lifespan and probably am on the downhill. Picking up speed, I might add. But I'm still here. I think about all the good friends and family who have added so much to our lives. One day, we are laughing and enjoying all those special days and even ordinary days, but then we must say goodbye. We knew we would do that at some point on the timeline, but we never thought it would come so soon or that they would be the ones to leave us behind.

I especially want to include the size six me, standing by the green 1970 Oldsmobile 442 W-30 car of my marine. What a glimpse back to our happy days when boy met girl, and we became one. The car wasn't too practical, especially because I didn't know how to shift the five speeds. I was perfectly okay with the car my dad helped me buy. It got me where I needed to be only forward and back.

I am finding it difficult to narrow down all the pictures of friends, family, and fun. Some have been with us from the days of lots of hair to none, from years of raising little ones to watching their grandchildren and ours have babies of their own. Now Michael and Subrina have added two more great-grandchildren, Sawyer and Lily. And Michele and Jake gave us Kaiden.

They went through many miscarriages and suffered through, but we know they will see their babies again when this life is through. We have shared our trials, joys, and pains, but what a beautiful picture of all our answered prayers.

The big table at Cracker Barrel in Kansas City, where we enjoyed so many laughs and memories with friends, gets smaller every year. And yet, life is sweeter the older we grow. We no longer fret about things that don't matter as we move along our lifespan clock.

Scripture tells us to store our treasures in heaven. For where our treasure is, there is our heart. Eternity is a far better investment in our lives. We will enjoy the people we have loved, have new pain-free bodies, do what we love doing, and never grow weary. There will be new things to discover and an eternity of using all the unused parts of our minds to enjoy sights, sounds, and adventures galore. Sign me up, Lord!

In the book of Revelation, it talks of the future heaven on earth. What God began in the book of Genesis, He will restore on this earth. And this time, we can't mess it up.

One thing I know: God never gives up, and He finishes everything He began. And that means you and me. The pictures of my life will include the lean years and the years I learned to trust. The in-between years, where His mercy and grace carried me when I needed Him the most.

This life picture will overlap with another special time. I want to include the very ecstatically happy mother-to-be me with the pictures of the children that have added such joy to the pages of why I am here.

The seasons come and the seasons go; good and hard times ebb and flow, but then we're stronger, and the things that really matter discard the things that never did.

I can't describe how grateful I have been that we got some things right. We let all the *not-so-important things* go and took that around the US tour to be with Grandma Peggy to celebrate with family and friends on her ninetieth birthday. What a beautiful thing to hear her say with tears in her eyes that it was the best day of her life!

We left New Hampshire, drove to Kansas City for a few days of R and R, and then we went north to Minnesota to pick up Don's brother Ronnie, who would not have gone if it had been anyone else but his mother.

Oh, the memories we would have missed if we had not taken that cross-country road trip to Idaho for the big surprise. Living all over the country has kept us from so many special events. When life's hectic pace seemed to suck out the oxygen in our family together times, our family didn't complain or blame.

Times are so different now. I can remember Christmas growing up when my family revolved around our neighborhood church. Everyone spent quality and quantity time singing and sharing. Stores were closed on Sundays, Christmas, Easter, and other important days so families could be together. I am grateful for the memories of my childhood when everyone that mattered lived within one hundred miles. But life is what it is, and we try the best we can. So with the days I have left, those allotted to me, I am resolved to do better—to listen more and talk less and whenever possible, be there for you.

If you are reading this, you have a copy of my book, *God Shed His Grace on Me*. I have been working on this story for over fifty years. Some of you don't have a clue why my life matters to you, but someone gave you a copy and perhaps it made you think. Maybe you will be inspired to leave your thoughts, life experiences, and the things that you would rather you or others did not repeat. Be honest, insightful, and delightful, and make it a good read. It's you, it's the you that you want others to meet.

So I return to the beginning of this epistle, for we have a brief moment in time to pass on what matters and why. Before you realize where time has gone, it's up. Did you do what you set out to do? Did you make a difference? Will anyone's life be influenced for the better by knowing about your life or mine?

Here are some tips that will help us all:

> Blessed is the one who does not walk in the counsel
> of the wicked or stand in the way of sinners or sit
> in the seat of mockers. But their delight is in the
> law of the Lord, and on his law they meditate day
> and night. They are like a tree planted by streams
> of water, which yields its fruit in season and whose
> leaf does not wither. Whatever they do will prosper.

This path of success is a promise for those who believe in God and know God. And you can know Him. He will make that happen, so accept the challenge, find a life worth living, and leave a legacy of faith to those who follow in your steps.

Now faith is being sure of what we
hope for and certain of what you do
not see. (Hebrews 11:1 NIV)

And without faith it is impossible to please
God because anyone who comes to him must
believe that he exists and that he rewards those
who earnestly seek him. (Hebrews 11:6)

I will quote Max Lucado again:

God didn't overlook your sins lest He endorse them. He didn't punish you, lest He destroy you. He instead found a way to punish the sin and preserve the sinner. Jesus took your punishment, and God gave you credit for Jesus's perfection.

Because of His great love for us, God, who is
rich in mercy, made us alive with Christ even
when we were dead in transgressions, it is by
grace you have been saved. (Ephesians 2:4–5)

Grace alone is not about how good we think we are or are not. It is not about who likes us or who rejects us, what group we belong to, or how much money we give to this cause or that. It is not about leaving this world with lots of applause or having no one of importance know our name, no color-guard, or even if we ever write a book, like me, that someone might read.

No, all those things may be good. They can be the result of a life well lived, but the salvation of the soul is unearned. It is a gift. Our merits merit nothing. God's work merits everything.

For God took on our flesh and came to earth. He came to die so we might live. And that is living a life worth living—to live our lives in a way that others will know Him. Knowing Him, they too will live!

And if you have never asked Him into your heart, why not ask Him right now? It is the best decision you will ever make.

Heavenly Father, I have sinned against You. I want forgiveness for all my sins. I believe Jesus died on the cross for me and rose again. Father, I give You my life to do with as You wish. I want Jesus Christ to come into my life and into my heart. I ask this in Jesus's name. Amen.

Final Thoughts

*Satisfy us in the morning with your unfailing
love, so that we may sing for joy to the end of our
lives. Give us gladness in proportion to our former
misery! Replace the evil years with good. Let us
see your miracles again; let our children see your
glory at work. And may the lord our God show
us his approval and make our efforts successful.
Yes make our efforts successful! (Psalm 91:1–2)*

The verse above is another one of my favorite verses from the Psalms. From the beginning of my story, I talked about my mom and dad being content. They were blessed, and they were satisfied with God's unfailing love. That is what is valuable in life. It is the peace that passes all understanding.

Evil is everywhere. I see the direction of this country, and my prayers have changed from "protect us" to "do what you need to do to bring this nation back to You." I do not want my children and grandchildren living under a repressive government, controlling everything they do. I want them to be free, free to reach their God-given potential.

I got this email from a friend back on September 29, 2012. I ran across it again and decided to put it in my final thoughts for the future generation.

Scary obituary:

> In 1887 Alexander Tyler, a Scottish history professor at the University of Edinburgh, had this to say about the fall of the Athenian Republic some 2,000 years prior; "A democracy is always tem-

porary in nature; it simply cannot exist as a permanent form of government. A democracy will continue to exist until the time that voters discover that they can vote themselves generous gifts from the public treasury. From that moment on, the majority always votes for the candidates who promise the most benefits from the public treasury, with the result that every democracy will finally collapse over loose fiscal policy, (which is) always followed by a dictatorship."

The average age of the world's greatest civilizations from the beginning of history, has been about 200 years. During those 200 years, these nations always progressed through the following sequence:

From bondage to spiritual faith; From spiritual faith to great courage; From courage to liberty;

From liberty to abundance;

From abundance to complacency; From complacency to apathy;

From apathy to dependence; This is about where America is Right Now in 2012 From dependence back into bondage. ("A Scary Obituary" by Alexander Tyler)

It is obvious to me that this is the way our country is heading. But if bondage is the only way to bring our nation back to God, then I am at peace with what I see. Who wins or loses elections is in God's hand. He uses it for His purpose. And He reminds me that all things work together for good to those who love Him and are called according to His purpose.

This is the story I want to tell. This is who I am, what I believe, and why. I want to define myself and not have the world define who I am. I want you to know our family history and pass it on.

I wrote my stories and thoughts to you, my children and grand-children, and those who have yet to be born. May God bless you and keep you. May His face shine down upon you and be gracious to you and give you peace.

I want to challenge you to live each day with the story you want others to read. The story that defines your character, what you value, and why it matters. For my story continues through all of you, and although your future is unknown, the Author of your lives knows the story He put in you.

And one day you will begin to notice a Scarlet Thread that has been running through the pages of your lives, and that is God's presence guiding you along His path. He is writing the story your life will tell, your legacy for those you love to follow. And it will be more than you could possibly know or understand right now, and maybe even a bestseller.

> It is never too late to be what you might have been. (George Elliot)

Let God rewrite your story, and there will be no end!

About the Author

Linda George lives with her husband, Don, in the beautiful Newfound Lake area of New Hampshire. She is the owner of Season's Country, an Airbnb surrounded by mountain views. Taking care of her flower and vegetable gardens and her guests is a beautiful way to appreciate her many blessings.

Her first publication appeared in the book *Walking with the Living God*. Her next writing assignment will be a series of letters written to her granddaughter that teach valuable life lessons based on stories from the Bible. The book will be titled *Principles and Promises to Payton*.

Along with enjoying her family and friends, she is actively involved in New Hampton Community Church. Currently, she is part of four Bible studies, two of which meet online. She has also been a children's Bible teacher for most of her life. Whatever the Lord leads her to do to help those in her community is a privilege and part of the many things she loves to do.

Linda wants to be a light in the darkness by bringing the good news of Jesus to those who do not know Him as their personal Lord and Savior. Her story can be an amazing inspiration for others who are seeking to know who He is and why He matters more than anything else we seek.

www.ingramcontent.com/pod-product-compliance
Lightning Source LLC
Chambersburg PA
CBHW031955160325
23481CB00002B/9